A Student's Guide to the Second Punic War at Advanced Level

By Peter Keating 2012©

Contents

Chapter One: The Causes of the Second Punic war 5
    How had this happened? 5
    The First Punic War 7
    Libyan revolt 9
    Hamiclar Barca and Spain 10
    Hannibal 11
    The system of government 14
    The Army 15
    Expansion of the Empire 15
Chapter Three: The Second Punic War Part 1 17
    Battle of the Ticinus River 19
    Sempronius and Sicily 20
    Gnaeus Cornelius Scipio in Spain 21
    Battle of the River Trebia December 218 21
    Lake Trasimene 24
    Fabius the Dictator 25
    The So-Called Battle of the Plain of Capua 26
    The Battles of Gereonium 27
    The Spanish Campaign of 217 28
    Spring Italy 216 BC 29
    The Battle of Cannae 2nd August 216 BC 29
Chapter Four: The Second Punic War Part Two 32
    The Aftermath of Cannae 32
    Rome goes on the Offensive 34
    Spain 216 35
    Spring Italy 215 36
    Sicily 215 37
    Spain 215 38
    Spring Italy 214 BC 39
    Sicily 214 40
    Greece 214 42

Spain 214	42
Italy 213 BC	43
Spain 213	44
Italy Spring 212	44
Sicily 212	46
Spain 212	47
Winter of 212	47
Chapter Five: The Second Punic War Part Three	**49**
Italy Spring 211	49
Sicily 211	51
Spain 211	51
Greece 211/210	52
Winter of 211/210	53
Italy 210	53
Sicily 210	54
Spain 210	55
Italy 209	55
Italy 208	58
Greece 208	59
Italy winter 208	60
Italy 207	60
Spain 207	62
Greece 207	62
Italy winter 207	63
Spring 206	63
Spain 206	65
Winter 206	67
Chapter Six End Game	**68**
Spring and Summer 205	68
Italy Spring 204	69
Carthage 204	70
Italy summer and autumn 204	71
Spring 203	71
Carthage 203	72
Liguria 203	73

- Bruttium summer 203 74
- Autumn Carthage 203 74
- Winter 203 74
- Spring 202 74
- Carthage 202 75
- Italy autumn 202 76
- Spring 201 76

Epilogue 78
- Appendix One 79

Bibliography 80

Chapter One: The Causes of the Second Punic war

The First Punic War, also known as the Sicilian War, (264-241 BC[1]) had left Rome as the new dominant sea power in the Western Mediterranean area; replacing the defeated Carthage. Rome now controlled the islands of Sicily, Sardinia and Corsica as part of its new developing empire outside of the Italian peninsula.

Carthage had been left excluded from the western Mediterranean; to compensate she expanded her colonies in modern Spain in an effort to rebuild her wealth.

How had this happened?

Carthage (meaning *New City*) was a colony of the Phoenician city of Tyre (Lebanon) and, according to Moscati (*1968*), its origins are clouded in legend. Virgil, writing at the same time as Livy, explains how Carthage became the ancient enemy of Rome after a prolonged stopover and a failed romance between the legendary founder of the Romans; Aeneas and the city's Queen Dido.[2]

By the 7th Century BC Carthage had expanded from the area around Carthage (modern Tunis in Tunisia); west along the North African coastline towards modern Gibraltar and east to Leptis Magna[3] in modern Libya. As with Tyre, Carthage expanded and setup colonies for the purpose of commerce and protecting trade routes. She then began to further develop her own colonies, such as Ibiza in the Balearic Islands, which provided a safe port between Carthage and the older Phoenician trading colonies on Sardinia. During this period Carthage is said to have either setup new colonies on Sicily, or taken over existing Phoenician settlements. By this time it is very probable that Carthage began to assert her independence from Tyre.

In response to the expansion of the Greek City state's colonies into Southern Italy and Sicily, they formed an alliance with the Etruscans (a dominant people in Italy in this period), in an effort to prevent or slow down this new invasion from the east. They were unsuccessful and were forced to retreat to the north western side of the island of Sicily; the Greek colonies were developed on the eastern side of the island. Carthage was also excluded from the coastline of Southern France, where the Greek city port of Massalia (Marseilles)[4] was founded by the Phocaeans, for example. For further details on the anti-Greek alliance and its importance in the Sixth century BC Mediterranean World see Moscati.

By the fourth Century BC Carthage had removed rule by a single dynasty, the Magonid, and replaced it with two magistrates (*Suffetes*) appointed by a Senate made up of 300 men chosen from

---

[1] I have used BC rather than BCE

[2] She committed suicide after he refused to stay with her in Carthage and continued with his mission to fight the Roman people in Italy

[3] See http://whc.unesco.org/en/list/183

[4] Where possible I have included the modern name of the classical site in brackets

the mercantile elite, with the Court of One Hundred (also picked from this class) and finally a general assembly of the citizens[5]. The senate mentioned here is the one later referred to as the Carthaginian Senate by both Polybius and Livy. As with Rome the elite of society now ruled in place of a king with the intention of never allowing a single person to dominate the state. Both cities were ruled by a form of oligarchy[6] government, which was designed to keep all power within a defined group of men drawn from each society; in Rome the Senatorial class and in Carthage the wealthiest merchant families (possibly those of the founding families).

Carthage returned to war with the Greeks over control of Sicily (406-367 BC), the main reason being geographic. The island of Sicily lies astride to Italy with the only entrances and exits from the western Mediterranean into the eastern Mediterranean. Carthaginian trade from its colonies in Libya and exports to the Levant were threatened by the presence of the Greeks on the island of Sicily. The result of the war left Carthage with control of the western third of the island.

Carthage in the fourth century came into contact with the newly expanding city state of Rome and treaties were signed. One treaty in 348 BC, mentioned by Polybius (2010), involved the agreement of Rome to recognise Carthaginian ascendancy in the western Mediterranean.

Following the conquests and death of Alexander the Great, Carthage again came under threat from the Greeks on Sicily after they formed an alliance with the newly created kingdom of Ptolemy based in Egypt. This kingdom held desires on Libya[7] and so shared an enemy in Carthage. Sicily became the scene of constant conflict for the Carthaginians; firstly against the leading Greek city of Syracuse, then against Pyrrhus of Epirus and following his dispatch of troops to the island in the wake of his invasion of southern Italy, came Graecia Magna to support fellow Greeks against Carthage. This brought Carthage into an alliance with Rome against Pyrrhus; for the first time two city states had a common enemy and cooperated.

Rome now dominated Southern Italy following the withdrawal of Pyrrhus; the majority of the Greek cities had allied themselves with Pyrrhus in the hopes of halting the Roman expansion. Conflict between the two powers was caused by a group of mercenaries left over from the war with Pyrrhus in southern Italy. They had moved onto the island of Sicily, captured Messana and situated themselves on the north east of the island opposite the southern Italian city and port of Rhegium. The mercenaries then came into conflict with Syracuse under its new leader Hiero.[8] By 265 BC Hiero had the upper hand and time was running out for the mercenaries; they needed an outside force who already distrusted the rising power of Hiero on Sicily to help them. Just to make sure they would have support they called on both Rome and Carthage to aid them. Carthage sent a small force to assist Messana, as it undermined Hiero's power and undermined their principle enemy on the island.

In Rome the Senate debated what measures they should take to support Messana; again they, like the Carthaginians, were considering the advantages of having a foothold on the island. Rome, as an expanding power in southern Italy, now saw the advantages of Sicily as it controlled access from the Western Mediterranean to the east and was wealthy in agricultural produce; the key to an

---

[5] Carthage, just like Rome, was heavily influenced by the Greek ideas of government

[6] Power of the few as opposed to democracy - the power of the people

[7] On the death of Alexander, his generals (and successors) divided up his empire among themselves and spent most of their time at war with each other.

[8] For more details on the First Punic War see Miles, 2011 and Bagnall, 2002

ancient economy. As an expanding city state Rome needed secure supplies of grain and Sicily was too good an opportunity to miss. So in 265 BC Rome and Carthage had similar strategic aims; control of the whole of Sicily.

The First Punic War

According to Polybius (2010) the Roman senate was deadlocked and called on the popular assembly to agree to support Messana realising that this would lead to conflict, at least with Hiero. Without doubt some senators were well aware that they would also be coming into conflict with Carthage over control of Messana. Rome began to prepare and so needed ships, which she asked of her new Italian-Greek allies; this quickly came to the attention of Carthage, who moved part of their powerful fleet into the straits of Messina under the command of Hanno. This was to block any Roman force attempting to cross from the mainland.

The Roman commander Consul Appius Claudius Caudex sent a small force to meet the mercenaries and persuaded them that Rome offered the best choice. In exchange for Roman support they needed to remove (i.e. kill) the Carthaginian garrison in their city. Claudius then attempted to send a small force across the strait, but Hanno and his ships defeated this force. Claudius attempted a second crossing in greater strength and this time succeeded. Hanno was forced to flee to the citadel within Messana, as Roman forces advanced into the city. Hanno was persuaded to remove his forces from the city in exchange for their lives, which he did, but Carthage saw this as cowardice and crucified him on his return to the city.

Rome now had a secure foothold on the island as well as a communication link with the mainland via the strait.

There were three main powers on the island now; Carthage in the West, Syracuse in the East and Rome at the north eastern tip of the island and they now came to blows over who controlled the island. So the First Punic war, or the Sicilian war, had begun; Carthage and Syracuse allied themselves against Rome. During attempts to stop the Romans reinforcing their position on the island, a Carthaginian Quinquereme[9] warship was taken intact by the Romans and quickly taken apart, teaching the Romans how to build warships as good as the best of Carthage. From this Rome was able to build a fleet that would eventually out-perform the Carthaginian's. The failure of Carthage and Syracuse to remove the Roman presence caused many of the Greek cities of the island to move to the Roman side.

In 263 BC Hiero followed the other Greek cities and joined the Roman side. The Carthaginians then failed to hold the port of Acragas, which gave the Romans the possibility of having a naval base on the island. By 260 BC the Romans had begun building a fleet of warships based on the captured model; firstly this was to deter raiding from Sardinia along the Italian coastline and secondly to attempt to defeat the Carthaginian dominance of the seas around Sicily. Part of the new yet untrained Roman fleet under the command of the consul Gnaeus Cornelius Scipio, was rashly rushed into action trying to defend the port of Lipara on the Aeolian Islands. They found themselves trapped in the harbour, were forced to surrender and their commander was captured. Scipio was ransomed

---

[9] Five banks of oars on each side of the warship; all the banks were used primarily in combat for speed while sails were used in normal movement.

and quickly forgiven by the Roman people as he made consul again in 254 BC. Later Hannibal[10], the commander of the Carthaginian fleet, after defeating Scipio decided to follow up on his victory by attacking Messana. A new consul, Duilius, had already arrived at Messana and the remaining fleet had undergone intensive training. Hannibal sailed straight into the remaining Roman fleet, which was on its way to intercept him, and he suffered a major defeat off the coast of northern Sicily close to Mylae. Sardinia and Corsica were now open to Roman raids and the Carthaginian fleets were now confined to the African side of the Mediterranean Sea.

On Sicily the Carthaginians had one major advantage; the Roman consular armies regularly changed consuls every year, whereas Carthaginians commanders were in their posts till they were either killed or sacked. This allowed Carthaginian commanders to build up their troops confidence regarding their leadership skills and, more importantly, it gave them time to dictate the tactics of the war with Rome –this amounted mainly to trying to avoid battles with consular armies. The consuls were desperate to prove their abilities so they needed combat to prove their worth, which meant they attacked each town and city one by one, sacking them if they were victorious, but in the process failing to defeat the Carthaginians in one great battle.

The Carthaginians lost few troops defending the towns and cities compared to Roman casualties that were heavier due to the haste of the consuls to take the towns by storm, rather than by siege. Secondly the Carthaginians conducted hit-and-run raids while holding on to the main city of Panormus and port of Lilybaeum (Marsala). As long as they held the major towns, cities and ports in the east of the island, the war was stalemated. The Carthaginian tactics could continue as long as they had enough money to pay for their mercenary armies to sit around most of the time, instead of fighting.

The Romans were not sitting around allowing Carthage to manage the war; in 256 BC they launched a massive invasion of North Africa using 330 ships under the joint command of the two consuls Lucius Vulso and Marcus Regulus. Carthage attempted to intercept the fleet, thus both fleets met close to cape Ecnomus (southern Sicily) and Rome again defeated the Carthaginian fleet. Once the defeat was known in Carthage, the people reacted to the news by pulling out most of their army from Sicily and bringing it home to defend the capital. Only Hamiclar was left on the island with a small force.

The Roman fleet landed at Cape Bon a short distance from Carthage. The army came ashore where it unexpectedly received orders not to attack Carthage at once, but to split the army up between the two consuls. Vulso and the majority of the army disembarked and returned to Italy. Rome had lost the advantage; Carthage gave the command of its forces to three commanders Hasdrubal, Boster and Hamiclar. Yet, they too failed to defeat the smaller Roman force; which in the meantime had taken Tunes (modern Tunis) and now laid siege to Carthage. Into this came the Numidians who, taking advantage of Carthage's predicament, also attacked the state.

At this point Regulus offered terms to Carthage to end the war. The terms amounted to Carthage relinquishing control of the western Mediterranean Sea and restricting itself to North Africa; releasing all Roman prisoners, paying for the war and lastly becoming an ally of Rome and paying annual tribute for the pleasure of being a friend.

It is at this point that Regulus' lack of troops made itself apparent; he was unable to storm the city or even maintain a land blockade. This allowed Carthage to bring in a new mercenary

---

[10] Hannibal, Hanno, Mago and Hasdrubal seem to have been common names among the Carthaginians

commander, the Spartan Xanthippus; who, during the siege, set about training the Carthaginian army in Spartan tactics. He then led the new army out of the city and defeated Regulus at Utica in 255 BC. Xanthippus returned home as he feared his new bosses were jealous of his success. The war entered another period of stalemate.

Rome again took the initiative in 254 and this time the consular armies undertook prolonged sieges and Panormus (Palermo) fell. Two years later Thermae Himerae and the Island of Lipara also fell to the new tactics. Hasdrubal led an attempt to retake Panormus but was defeated by Metelus and on his return to Carthage, was executed. The last major stronghold of Carthage on Sicily was the port city of Lilybaeum and Rome laid siege by land and sea to the city from 250 BC onwards.

Now Carthage's reliance on imports began to make itself felt. Sicily had been its major source of income and food; with the blockade of Lilybaeum, all revenue and food came to a halt from the island. The city now had a major problem of how to pay for the war on Sicily. It had also sent Hanno out with an army to begin to secure the hinterland and stretches of the North African coastline following the recent Numidian attacks. Carthage now found itself with two wars to fight and the one on its doorstep took precedent over Sicily. Hamiclar Barca (lightning or flash) was given the difficult task of fighting a limited war with Rome, until Hanno had completed his campaign. Hanno extended Carthage's inland territory to the towns of Tebessa (in modern Algeria) and Sicca (El Kef).

Hamiclar's first task on arriving on the island was to regain control of the mercenary army, which had quickly revolted once no pay had arrived from Carthage. Once in control he adopted hit-and-run tactics, avoiding facing a Roman army in the open and instead hitting towns and villages. Doing this he intended to force the Romans to deploy more troops inland away from the siege of Lilybaeum. He also ensured that all his raiding was reported in Carthage and built himself quite a reputation as a fearless fighter against Rome. Expanding his mission he took control of Monte Castelacio close to Panormus and from there raided the countryside. This tied down more Roman forces in an effort to contain him in one place, but it also restricted his actions as he was now hemmed into one area. This was also a reflection of his true position on the island, as his pin pricks on the Romans only emphasised how incapable he was of regaining control of Sicily for Carthage. In 244 he took the old Carthaginian settlement of Eryx (Erice) after abandoning his position on Castelacio. But he left the Roman garrison still on the mountain top. The end result was that he became surrounded by the Romans from the summit and the plain around his position half way up the mountain.

The Romans now began the last phase of the war; rebuilding its navy in preparation for a final showdown with the Carthaginian fleet. To draw the Carthaginian fleet out they tightened their grip around Lilybaeum and on the only other Carthaginian position; the town of Drepana (Trapani). In 241 BC the fleets clashed close to the islands of the Aegates (Aegadian Islands), leaving Carthage without any means to support its last two positions on the island. Secondly, she could no longer afford the cost of the war with Rome as she was still dealing with the Numidians and so sued for peace with Rome.

The terms Rome offered were the same as Regulus had offered; she was to abandon Sicily, Sardinia and Corsica. She was to pay for the cost of the war at 2,200 talents of silver over the next twenty years. The terms were swiftly changed by Rome after the people voted to increase the fine to 3,200 talents. Carthage had no choice but to agree and the task was given to Hamiclar Barca as he was still on the island. He saved himself from the disgrace by giving the actual negotiations to the commander of Lilybaeum, Gisco.

Libyan revolt

The main problem for Carthage was what to do with the mercenary army still in Sicily; they no longer had enough money, after paying Rome, to pay the outstanding wages. Under the terms they had to remove all their forces, so they were shipped back to Carthage. Hamilcar, seeing the danger, resigned his command before he left the island of Sicily. The Carthaginian senate had the mercenary army dispatched to Sicca with a promise of pay to follow. Quickly the mercenary army revolted as they realised they weren't going to be paid; they elected their own commanders and marched on Tunes and held it to ransom. Gisco was sent by the senate with some money with the intention of dividing up the rebels by nationality and paying one nation, thus, hopefully, causing the others to attack them. Instead the rebels took and sacked Utica, defeating a small Carthaginian force under Hanno and then marched into Libya; where an uprising had been simmering over their treatment by Carthage as cash cows.

In 240 Sardinia revolted and it appears to have been connected to the Libyan revolt. This time Carthage was unable to intervene and so lost control of the mineral rich island. In 238 Rome annexed the island, breaking its treaty with Carthage in the full knowledge that Carthage had its hands full and couldn't oppose Rome at the present. To add insult to injury, Rome then demanded more talents of silver.

The Libyan revolt continued and, with the aid of the mercenary army, were able to besiege Carthage. It was at this point that Hamilcar Barca came to his city's aid and, with a smaller force and 2,000 Numidian cavalry, he defeated the rebels; feigning a retreat which caused the rebels to advance after his troops. As they broke ranks he reeled around to crush them with his cavalry from the flanks as his forces advanced into the mêlée. The revolt was finally ended in 237 after Hanno and Hamilcar finally agreed to co-operate, thereby defeating the rebels they extracted a very harsh revenge on the defeated.

Hamilcar Barca and Spain

Following the end of the First Punic war and the revolt, Carthage appears to have undergone a change in its system of government. The public assembly and the middle class (merchants, junior officers) wrenched power away from the senate, thereby removing their right to appoint commanders of the army, then forcing the senate to allow them to debate matters of state and approving them by popular vote. Hamilcar seems to have been well aware of this shift of power and used the wealth he had accumulated during the revolt to buy votes for himself in the assembly. He put this to good use when the senate had to decide how to rebuild Carthage. Hanno and his supporters favoured further expansion in North Africa, while Hamilcar and his supports in the senate and assembly favoured expanding into Spain. The assembly voted in favour of Hamilcar and he was appointed to command an army and any newly conquered land in Spain. He also paid for his own mercenary army to accompany him into Spain.

Spain had ample sources of gold and silver, as well as land suitable for agriculture and it was controlled by numerous independent Celtic tribes. Hamilcar was unable to sail to Spain and instead walked along the North African coastline crossing somewhere close to modern Gibraltar. He quickly began conquering the region of the Sierra Morena with its silver mines which, according to Miles (2011), was the main reason for the move into Spain. During the first year 237 BC he started minting silver coins. He expanded along the southern coastline founding a new city Acra Leuce (close to

Alicante). The minting of his own coins may well be a sign that he saw Spain as his own personal fiefdom independent from Carthage, but he paid tribute to the city, sending back enough silver to enable the city to pay off the Romans in the agreed time.

Hamiclar then advanced further into Spain; picking off one tribe at a time, then making personal alliances with the defeated tribe. He expanded his army, recruiting from the newly conquered tribes to enable him to take on the next tribe. Following the death of Hamiclar the army elected its next commander; his son-in-law Hasdrubal. This was a complete break with Carthaginian tradition, as the senate was expected to appoint or remove commanders. The senate and assembly, now controlled by Bacrid supporters, acquiesced to this by voting their approval. The Bacrids were now free to set their own policies in Spain without hindrance from Carthage while still nominally allies of the city. Hasdrubal continued with Hamiclar's polices in Spain; annexing more territory and bringing in old Phoenician and Greek settlements into his growing empire. The empire was based on a system of personal alliances to the Bacrid family not to Carthage; tribute was paid in silver, gold and produce along with an annual levy of men for the army. He founded the city of New Carthage (Qast-Hadasht) in 227 BC as the capital of his empire.

Rome was brought into Spain by the Greek colony of Massalia (Marseilles), who feared the growing size of Bacrid Spain would interfere with their trade with Spain. Rome first approached Hamiclar in 231 BC and he is reported by Polybius (2010) to have stated his intention was to use Spain to help pay off the debts to Rome paid in full by 228 BC. Rome again sent a Senatorial delegation to New Carthage in 228 BC to delineate the areas of influence between Rome and Bacrid Spain, which was set on the River Ebro; this resulted with both parties agreeing not to send armies over the river. What makes this important is that the Romans already recognised that Spain was separate from Carthage and so sent the delegation there; not to Africa. It made more sense to speak to the real power instead of pretending that Carthage had any control in Spain[11]. In 221 BC Hasdrubal was assassinated by a member of the army and they (the army) elected the son of Hamiclar, Hannibal Barca aged 26 to take over; once again Carthage agreed to this. Spain was now being ruled by a dynasty; the Bacrids were now emperors in all but name.

Hannibal

We have very little real information on the personality of Hannibal, instead we are left, for example, with Polybius Book 3's (Polybius, 2010) brief outline which Livy in Book XXI (Livy, 1965) enlarges on as part of his explanation of how a barbarian was able to outwit and defeat Roman armies during the 2nd Punic war.

Briefly they portray a man driven by his father's hatred for Rome, which he was made to swear to follow at the age of Nine; an 'Unremitting hatred for the Romans' as Polybius reports (Polybius, 2010). Both authors agree that fortune favoured him more often than it did the Romans and they both agree he was an outstanding military commander. Livy then goes on to show that even with these Roman-like qualities he was a barbarian as he didn't keep his word, was the cruellest of the Carthaginians and gave quite a complaint as to how the Roman's treated non-citizens in this period. For Livy he uses his characterisation of Hannibal as the nemesis of his hero, the young Publius

---

[11] It may well be that Spain was treated as collective colony of Carthage, with independence as long as it paid tribute

Cornelius Scipio (Africanus), so the character is built up by Livy, but already prepared for his eventual fall at the hands of the young Roman patriot Scipio at the close of the war.

We can assume that Hamiclar and Hasdrubal both trained Hannibal in the arts of war, government and diplomacy. For a modern treatment of the character of Hannibal see Miles (2011). Hannibal's tactics during the 2nd Punic war point to his having learnt well from his father; in always picking the location of the battle and trying to avoid direct confrontation with a Roman army; instead using any means to break up the Roman military formations which had proved more adaptable in combat than Carthaginian or Greek phalanxes.

Once Hannibal was elected he set out to complete the conquest of Spain, finishing off the remaining Celtiberian tribes; we can assume that he also began preparations for his land assault on Rome. He was successful in his operations against the tribesmen and proved to his men that he was a very capable leader. Livy in book XXI (1965) offers the portrait that he slept less than his men, wore the simple military clothing of an officer and even slept in his cloak on the ground; just as the men did.

So why did he start the war with Rome? Livy and Polybius agree that it was the assault on Saguntum; the only city within his sphere of control that was allied to Rome, which triggered the war for Rome. Hannibal, if he was to launch a successful invasion of Rome, needed to ensure that the Roman's had no allies in Spain with which to cooperate and cut him off from his main supply base. So the city was doomed. Hannibal probably hoped that the appearance of his army outside of the city would have been enough to cause the city to surrender to him (Hook, 2005). Instead the city expected a Roman fleet to appear and break the siege, so they held out for as long as it took Hannibal to prepare his attack on the city, which was about 8 months. Hannibal adopted standard siege tactics: sealing off the city, undertaking mining operations against the most suitable wall and having his siege engineers build the necessary equipment to allow his army to break into the city. To keep his army busy he had them regularly launch attacks. Once inside the city his men were allowed to pillage at will (a form of bonus for winning), which was the standard fate of any city that fell following a siege. For Hannibal it allowed him to collect gold and silver from the city's treasury which would assist in paying for the coming campaign. Lastly Rome no longer had an ally in Spain.

But it would appear that Rome may have actually caused the war by its actions after the end of the 1st Punic War; when it broke the treaty with Carthage, took over Sardinia and Corsica and extended the size of the fine. Polybius, in Book 3 (2010), remarks that Hannibal, when discussing his actions at Saguntum with the Roman envoys, would have been justified if he had used those actions as his reasons for acting against the city. Instead he gave a spurious excuse concerning Roman interference in the city and Carthage's right to help those under oppression. Without doubt he wanted war and all he needed to do now was drag Carthage into the conflict, to ensure that he could count on them for political and military support when he needed it. Lastly, to ensure the full support of Carthage and any other enemies of Rome he needed the Romans to declare war on him, as this would put his enemies in Carthage on the defensive and also announce to the world that Rome had a new enemy.

Would a better question be; was war with Rome inevitable for Hannibal? The answer would be **Yes**, as all the classical authors agree that Hannibal was born to avenge his father and Carthage's humiliation at the hands of Rome following its defeat in the 1st Punic war. He followed his father and brother-in-law in building up the Spanish empire to act as paymaster for the future war they envisioned they would launch on Rome. As it happened the moment came whilst Hannibal was in command.

As already mentioned Rome made no effort to find accommodation with Carthage following the end of the war. For a historical parallel, consider the treatment of Germany at the end of World War One and the harsh impositions laid on the country by the Treaty of Versailles; such as the loss of territory, having to pay reparations and collective guilt. The treatment of defeated Germany is considered to be one of the contributing factors leading to the Second World War.

Chapter Two: Rome between the Wars

For Rome, victory in the First Punic War allowed her to begin to develop an empire. New colonies were established in Southern Italy in an effort to Romanise the local Greek Italians, which must have caused a little laugh to the people who brought civilisation to Italy in the first place. More importantly the Greek cities in the south now found that their new Roman allies were expensive to have. They were not only taxed by Rome (Roman citizens didn't pay direct taxes, so needed the income the new allies generated for them), but they were expected each year to produce a levy of infantry from their population and from the rich a levy of cavalry. This might well be bearable in normal times, but in times of crisis it could become burdensome.

As Rome expanded outside its old frontiers, the system of colonies became its prime method for introducing the Roman system to its new empire. As in Southern Italy, Sicily began to be colonised by Rome, which was acceptable in the Carthaginian part of the island, but encroachments close to Syracuse and other so-called independent cities may well have caused some concern; mainly as to how long it would be before they became colonies of Rome themselves.

For the first time Rome now controlled territory outside of the Italian peninsula, as well as controlling the western Mediterranean thanks to the sea victories over Carthage. Internally her system of government evolved to cope with the developing empire.

The system of government

Rome was made up of two types of citizens; the elite patrician class and the plebs. The patrician class was, in turn, made up of the aristocracy (those who claimed direct descent from the founding families of Rome) and the equestrian order. The plebs were literally everyone else, from a wealthy merchant to a beggar. Those who became wealthy aimed to move from the plebeian class and gain entry into the patrician class. The normal method was, for those wealthy enough, to run for election as a magistrate; normally after completing a military career with the rank of tribune. Rome had been governed by a system of elected magistrates, which were mainly drawn from the elite of Roman society; therefore within the patrician class.

The only real path for social promotion was to enter the elections for the lowest level of magistrate, the Quaestor, at the age of 30; the post was unpaid, yet any task needed was paid for by the magistrate and like every magistrate the post was for one year only. Election was by the Comitia tribute (an assembly of the plebs) and this again required wealth; as the easiest method of election was to buy votes. The highest office that could be reached was Consul; with two elected each year. But as a candidate worked their way up the system, the chances of being chosen to sit in the senate increased and this would place them in the patrician class. If you reached the level of Praetor, you would gain your first command of a Roman army. Following the First Punic War two more Praetors were elected for the role of ruling over Sicily and Sardinia.

The role of the two consuls was to command all the armies assigned to campaign within any region the senate decided required their presence; they had to be at least forty-two years of age. By this point they would already have had quite an extensive military career. The normal process was for one consul to rule alternate months if both were still in Rome. If one was away on campaign the other undertook their ceremonial religious role as well, also presiding over assemblies and the senate. In the event of a major crisis the senate could elect one of their own, who had already served as a consul, to the role of dictator who normally served for 6 months and had complete authority over all the assemblies, law courts and armies during this period.

The Army

The Roman army of this period was recruited annually from the citizen body; the minimum qualification for service was that the citizen owned property worth 400 denarii and was aged between 17 and 46 yrs. Service was for a maximum of 16 years for a foot soldier and ten years for a cavalryman (*eques*). These figures represent the maximum period that the soldier would be required to report for duty each year. In times of crisis they were kept on active duty. Rome recruited enough men annually to be able to field four legions; about a maximum of 20,000 men. The legion was made up of four different types of soldier; the *Velites* were recruited from the poorest and youngest and were lightly equipped skirmishers, these formed a screen in front of the legion. Next was the first line of heavy infantry; the *hastate* made up of the next age and wealth group, placed in maniples of 120 men and equipped with swords, the heavy shield the *scutum,* and spears. Next in line were the *princeps;* those in the prime of life equipped in the same fashion as the *hastate*. Lastly was the third rank; the *triarii* made up the senior and oldest draftees. The officer class was normally drawn from the cavalry, as they were wealthier and needed to serve at least ten years before they could be chosen normally by a consul or assemblies of the plebs to be a military tribune.[12]

Expansion of the Empire

From 230 BC onwards till 223 BC Rome conducted military operations on the islands of Sardinia and Corsica, subduing the interior tribes. In conjunction with these operations the senate ordered the consuls from 227 onwards to campaign north of Etruria and Umbria, (which marked the frontier of northern Italy) into the region known as *Gallia Cisalpina,* or Gaul this side of the Alps (Cisalpine Gaul). Mainly they campaigned against the Gallic tribes located on and south of the River Po. In 232 BC one of the tribune of the plebs (the only magistrate to represent the plebs to the senate), Gaius Flaminius, proposed a law giving grants of land to citizens and retired soldiers taken from these defeated tribes. The main reason was to encourage Romans to live in these new lands and gradually either push out the locals, or convert them into Roman allies; secondly it also helped to solve the continual problem of land shortages for the peasants and farmers around Rome. The knock on effect was to convince the Gaul's that the Romans had only one intention; that of stealing their land.

This alienated them and the majority of Gallic tribes remained hostile to the Romans. Within ten years a major conflict broke out between a group of tribes and Rome. As the conflict expanded, Gallic tribes from outside the region were encouraged to join in. Rome in 226 BC felt so threatened that they buried alive two Gauls and two Greeks in the Forum Boerium, as called for by a prophecy to avert the fall of Rome. In 225 BC the Gallic tribes advanced into Etruria and defeated a Roman army at Faesulae (Fiesole), later in the year a twin consul army defeated them at Telamon. For the

---

[12] For further reading on the development of the Roman Army see (Keppie, 1998)

next five years Roman armies campaigned again in the Po Valley, slowly bringing the region back under Roman control. In 219 BC two new colonies were founded at Placentia (Piacenza) and Cremona, marking the return of the region south of the Po to Roman control.

Earlier in 229 BC Rome had also begun operations in the Balkans; in a region known as Illyria, with both consuls leading armies. One of the consuls went up against one of the local rulers, who had been attacking Corcyra on the Dalmatian coast and the other with the remaining army marching into Epirus (completing unfinished business from before the First Punic War). The campaign was successful and the Illyrians were forced to agree to terms and pay for the cost of the war. Several cities along the Dalmatian coast, including Corcyra, allied themselves with Rome, thus securing the coastline opposite Italy.

In 220 BC a revived Macedon, under Antigonus Donson, began to fear the Roman presence in Illyria that he regarded as within his sphere of influence. So he made an alliance with Demetrius of Pharos, who then seized power in Illyria and, with encouragement, launched attacks against Rome's Dalmatian allies. In 219 BC both consuls; one of whom was Lucius Aemilius Paullus, campaigned against Demetrius forcing him to flee into Macedon. Rome had now gained a firm foothold in the Balkans and may well have been contemplating further campaigns against Macedon for intervening in Roman affairs.

Rome had shown that she could now conduct two campaigns at the same time; one in Sardinia and another in the Po Valley. The army was able to conduct these without problems and then be able to switch to a different location to conduct a shorter campaign when necessary. Rome's senate and its population had seen nothing but success following the defeat of Carthage; so the army and its commanders had grown very confident in their abilities, formations and the system of yearly consular commanders.

Chapter Three: The Second Punic War Part 1

In 219 BC a delegation from Saguntum reached Rome and asked for military support against Hannibal's siege of the city. The senate debated the issue, but in light of the on-going conflict in Illyria it was unable to dispatch forces to support the city. Instead it resorted to diplomacy in the vain hope that this would save the city and Rome's reputation in Spain as a safe and reliable ally. Senior senators P V Flaccus and Q B Tamphilus were sent to Spain to issue Hannibal with a stern warning of Roman's displeasure over his actions. Livy (1965) states the demands were essentially that not only was the siege to end, but Hannibal was to pay reparations to Saguntum. Hannibal had no intention of giving in to Rome's demand and to show his contempt for Rome, he kept them waiting until it suited him to see them.

Hannibal refused their demands.

The senators travelled to Carthage with similar demands, along with the demand that they (Carthage) hand over Hannibal to them as a war criminal. Livy (1965) relates how it is only Hanno the enemy of the Bacrids who speaks wisely and suggests that Carthage acceded to the demands. The rest of the senate were, of course, with Hannibal and they voted against Hanno and Rome's demands. The senators returned to Rome with the response that was probably expected and by sending the delegation Rome had gained time in which to conclude the conflict in Illyria.

In 218 BC the plebeian assemblies in Rome voted for war with Carthage and Hannibal, giving the senate the power it needed to begin preparations for the conflict. The senate raised 6 legions, 50% more than normal, extra cavalry and a levy of more troops from her Italian allies. They also sent a delegation made up of the ex-consuls Q Fabius, M Livius, L Aemilius, G Licinius and Q Baebius to Carthage to officially declare war on the city. It also gave the city one last chance, in light of the growing preparations for war in Rome, to accept their terms as presented earlier. Carthage accepted the declaration of war, the delegation returned via Spain and Gaul in an effort to build up allies ready for the war with Hannibal. This failed as the Spanish did not trust Rome (according to Livy (1965)) following the fall of Saguntum and the Gauls regarded the Romans as their natural enemies.

The senate then directed the consul for the year, P Cornelius Scipio, to take 2 legions; 2000 cavalry, and 14,000 allied infantry to Spain and begin operations against Hannibal. The other consul, T Sempronius, was given the same size force and dispatched to Sicily; to make preparations for an invasion of Carthage and bring the war to a swift end by the end of the year. The praetor, Lucius Manlius, with the remaining 2 legions, cavalry and 14,000 allied troops was sent to Cisalpine Gaul to guard the frontier with Gaul in case the tribes would take advantage of Rome's new war.

At the same period Hannibal left Gades (Cadiz) on the Atlantic coast of Spain, after offering sacrifice at the old Phoenician religious settlement and re-joined his army at New Carthage. He began the march towards Northern Italy in the early spring. In the meantime he dispatched agents into Gaul to prepare the route for his army. They needed to buy supplies and to do this they brought the loyalty of the local tribes, which had the added benefit that Hannibal would not only be supplied, but be advancing unopposed, as well as having local guides to speed his journey.

He left a part of his army, made up of North Africans (as they were not native they were less likely to join a local revolt) with his brother Hasdrubal to guard Spain against revolt and Roman attacks. He understood that without Spain, he had no secure base from which to receive supplies of men and money. Hannibal took the Spanish with him, also sending some to stiffen the defence of Carthage[13]. As well as enforced with the task of taking Lilybaeum from Rome, which he probably saw as a "just" revenge for his father's failure to hold the port, and so restored Carthage's presence back on the island. Secondly he may have hoped that Hiero of Syracuse might change sides and join him against Rome. This enabled Hannibal to shorten his lines of communication and receive supplies from Carthage via Sicily for his invasion of Italy.

On crossing the Ebro River he officially entered Rome's agreed area of influence and began the war with Rome. According to Livy (1965) he began his march with 90,000 infantry, 12,000 cavalry and probably with a larger number of camp followers; made up of slaves, baggage train, supplies, and families. After crossing the Pyrenees he left Hanno with a force probably made up from the group Livy (1965) claims refused to go any further into Gaul to guard the entrance into Spain from Gaul. According to Polybius (2010) he left half the baggage train with Hanno, which made more sense than bringing all those extra mouths with him.

During the spring in Cisalpine Gaul two tribes; the Boii and Insubrains, revolted against Rome over the setting up of the two colonies of Placentia and Cremona in the Po valley. The Roman settlers were attacked and fled from Placentia to the safety of the older colony of Mutina. The Gauls then surround the town, but were unable to storm it. The praetor, L Manlius, was diverted from his mission at the frontier of Gaul to go to the aid of the colony. He failed to scout the route properly and was continually ambushed by the Gauls until he reached the territory of the Brixian; a tribe still allied to Rome and from there he reached Tannetum (Taneto) on the Po, where he awaited supplies and support from the Adriatic coast.

When news of the uprising, followed by the sloppy actions of Manlius, arrived in Rome it caused alarm. The senate was forced to change its plans for Cornelius Scipio, instead of heading on to Spain he had to hand over one of his new legions and 5,000 allied troops to the praetor Gaius Atilius, who was dispatched hurriedly to support Manlius and bring an end to the revolt. For Rome the revolt had come at the worst moment, they had already raised extra forces to deal with Hannibal and Carthage and now they were going to have to raise a seventh legion and levy another 5,000 troops from her allies. Already their plans to deal with the threat had come unstuck without even coming to blows with Hannibal.

Cornelius Scipio was delayed in sailing while he raised the new forces. Eventually he landed at Massilia (Marseilles) and learnt the news that Hannibal had left Spain and was in Gaul, presumably advancing towards his location. For Cornelius Scipio this was either terribly bad timing (in which case he could retreat back to Cisalpine Gaul) or a great opportunity to intercept Hannibal before he could reach Cisalpine Gaul. Cornelius Scipio saw the advantage and the prestige he could gain, not only for himself, but his family and Rome and decided to intercept Hannibal. He sent out half his cavalry north along the east bank of the Rhône to try and locate Hannibal, whom he understood was now close to the river.

Hannibal was, in fact, much closer than Cornelius Scipio suspected and was attempting to cross the Rhône further up. He had been held up by a local tribe; the Volcae, who refused to let him pass through their territory. So he sent another Hanno; the son of Bomiclar with a force of cavalry to cross the river further up and then come around behind the Volcae, attacking them from behind as

---

[13] Following the declaration of war with Rome, Hannibal and Carthage now worked actively together

Hannibal began his crossing of the Rhône. The result was a successful crossing and defeat of the tribe, Livy gives a wonderful fictional account of the crossing and battle in Book XXI (1965).

Shortly after the crossing of the Rhône, Cornelius Scipio's cavalry clashed with a smaller force of Numidian cavalry undertaking a similar mission for Hannibal. The first clash was a victory for Rome and increased the confidence of Cornelius Scipio, who on hearing the news, set off after Hannibal with the intent of bringing him into battle. By the time he reached the crossing point, Hannibal had a head start of at least three days and was marching north away from the coast.

It is at this point when the question can be asked "did Hannibal intend from the start to cross into Cisalpine Gaul along the coast? Or to cross using the passes in the Alps?" The answer is; we don't know because we have no historical records, or even a Carthaginian equivalent Polybius or Livy to give Hannibal's side of the conflict. All the evidence is drawn from the Roman side and so it is biased, which makes asking questions like this pertinent as it reminds us that we don't know the story from Hannibal's side. So it allows historians, starting with Polybius (who uses this only occasionally) onwards and including Livy (who makes extensive use of these made up speeches) to try and answer this. They normally follow the custom of Thucydides (where he wasn't a witness to the event), who gives the main actors in his history speeches to explain to the reader what he thought they were thinking and what he thought their later actions were based on. So we have Hannibal, all through Livy's account, giving all these marvellous speeches to encourage his troops, but also to explain to the reader why he was undertaking these and later actions.

What all the classical writers do agree on is that Hannibal avoided battle with Cornelius Scipio in Gaul. Instead he took his men up into the Alps and spent, according to Livy (1965), 15 days crossing into Northern Italy and in the process lost perhaps half of his original army.

It is at this point that Cornelius Scipio made the most important decision of the whole of the Second Punic War; he sent his brother Gnaeus Scipio with the majority of his army on into Spain. Why was this such an important decision? Cornelius, by doing this, cuts Hannibal off from his logistical base of Spain. He also places a large Roman force in Spain, right in the heart of the Bacrid Empire. The action would not bear fruit for a number of years, but it can be seen as a game changer. Hannibal could no longer retreat back out of Italy and was now confined there. His brother would have difficulty supporting him, while trying to deal with the Roman force. Carthage now had to decide who would get vital supplies and who was more important; Spain or Hannibal, remembering that Rome at the start of the War controlled the sea routes.

Battle of the Ticinus River

Cornelius Scipio, with his remaining force, embarked and sailed probably to Genoa. On learning that Hannibal had successfully crossed the Alps and entered the region, moved his forces up to Placentia and picked up the two praetor's forces to add to his smaller force probably in October 218 BC. On learning that Hannibal was advancing eastwards north of the Po, he decided to intercept Hannibal before he crossed the river Ticinus and so defend Placentia and Cremona from his advance. Cornelius Scipio reached the river, first building a bridge and moved his army onto the west bank, thereby blocking Hannibal's advance. Livy (1965) introduces both commanders and their supposed motives by having them give speeches, and in Hannibal's case having captured Gauls fight for their freedom. Then both commanders sent out a large force of cavalry to locate each other's main force.

They spotted each other; Cornelius Scipio placed his Velites in the front alongside the Gallic allied cavalry to act as a screen for his main cavalry force moving behind this front rank. Hannibal moved in one solid line with his Gallic allies in the centre and his Numidians cavalry on either wing. It seems, using both Livy and Polybius' accounts, that Hannibal's forces charged en mass causing the Velites to flee back into the second line of Roman cavalry, making them unable to mount a proper charge without running over their own men. The Numidians quickly outflanked the Roman forces and attempted to squeeze them into a confined space. During this Cornelius Scipio was wounded and according to Livy (1965) was rescued by his son, while Polybius (2010) fails to mention this incident regarding Scipio the younger.

Whatever happened to Cornelius, he ordered a retreat and what was left of the Roman force retreated back to the rest of the army. Cornelius Scipio now acted irrationally and ordered his army to rapidly retreat back over the Ticinus; so fast was the retreat, that the men assigned to guard the bridge were left behind attempting to destroy it. Mago and the cavalry were sent by Hannibal (his most experienced cavalry commander) and on finding the Roman camp empty, advanced to the river trying to locate the Roman army. At this point they captured the Roman rear-guard trying to demolish the bridge. Cornelius Scipio retreated all the way back to Placentia, leaving the region behind undefended. After setting up a standard marching camp, he allowed Mago to cross the Po and began harassing him. During this period his Gallic allies deserted him, as he was no longer defending their lands. His army must also have suffered a massive loss in morale at the defeat and constant retreat, as well as the faith in their commander who was responsible.

Sempronius and Sicily

While Cornelius Scipio was in southern Gaul, Sempronius and his forces reached Sicily, coinciding with Hannibal's forces operating out of Carthage beginning their attack on Sicily. For Carthage the operation started bad; the diversionary attack aimed at northern Sicily ran into Hiero's fleet in the Straits of Messana and were destroyed. This meant that Carthage was not going to have Syracuse as an ally at this point in the war. The main Carthaginian fleet approached Lilybaeum and were routed by the Roman fleet stationed there. Sempronius dispatched part of his fleet to Malta to retake the island, which they did, bringing back the garrison including its commander. Sempronius and the rest of the fleet reached Lilybaeum ready for the assault on Carthage. In the port he held a public auction of the captives; probably making quite profit for himself and a bonus for the army. According to Livy (1965) Sempronius did not undertake the attack on Carthage; as a small raiding party of Carthaginian ships were causing problems along the southern Italian coastline around Vibo (Vibo Valentia). So he dispatched his fleet to protect the coastline, probably in October.

It is at this point that the senate, on hearing of Cornelius Scipio's defeat at the hands of Hannibal, ordered Sempronius to bring his army back and go to the aid of Scipio at Placentia. It is more than likely that the senate also called off the attack on Carthage and recalled Sempronius at the same time. Sempronius then dispatched his army to Ariminum close to the mouth of the Po, while he sailed directly for Rome. He divided up his fleet between his second command with orders to block any Carthaginian ships approaching the Italian coastline, northern Sicily and surrounding islands; with around fifty ships given to the commander of Sicily the praetor Aemilius based at Lilybaeum. According to Polybius (2010) Sempronius' army reached Ariminum (Rimini)[14] after 40 days hard march. He then joined his army and they marched to Placentia, and then on to where Cornelius had

---

[14] Unless otherwise stated modern Italian places names obtained from (Multo, 2012)

relocated his army to a position along the eastern bank of the River Trebia, probably in late November or early December.

Gnaeus Cornelius Scipio in Spain

Gnaeus Scipio landed at Empúries meeting no resistance, probably in the early autumn of 218 BC. Using his fleet he raided along the coast down to the river Ebro, in the process he gained a number of towns and tribes who willingly changed sides. Those that did not change were besieged and taken. Hanno reacted to the invasion and clashed with Gnaeus at Cissa (close to Tarraco), there he was defeated and captured along with his Celtiberian ally Andobales and the baggage left behind earlier by Hannibal. Hasdrubal, on hearing the news brought his forces across the Ebro and caught a force of Romans by surprise, scattering them. Then he retired with his army back to New Carthage to await the spring. Gnaeus and his forces wintered at Tarraco (Tarragona); Rome had fought its first successful campaign in Iberia.

Battle of the River Trebia December 218

Rome had now deployed a joint consular army along the river Trebia, and such was the crisis now engulfing Rome that they expected their consuls and army to continue campaigning into the winter. This was unusual; not only because the weather conditions made movement more difficult, but because the citizen makeup of the army also expected to have been at home, already preparing the land after collecting the harvest and this included the allied forces. The joint command seems to have failed as Cornelius Scipio was still wounded and unable to command properly with Sempronius, who seemed to have taken over completely. For both consuls they too expected to be in Rome and trying to have themselves re-elected in the forthcoming consular elections in the New Year of 217 BC. With this added pressure Sempronius, against Cornelius's advice, decided to attempt to recover their Gallic allies by putting pressure on Hannibal and forcing him to keep his forces together. Hannibal in the meantime, apart from harassing Scipio's forces, had set about gaining allies and punishing those, like the Boii, who still remained on the fence. Sempronius, after receiving an appeal from the Gauls, sent a force of cavalry and Velites into their land to chase off Hannibal's cavalry who were harassing the Gauls on the west bank of the Trebia. This force, after crossing the river, quickly found a raiding party and chased them all the way back to Hannibal's camp, where both sides clashed. Scipio sent support from the Roman camp, Hannibal only enough to stop his forces collapsing. The result was a draw; as both sides were able to withdrawal unhindered from the battle site.

Sempronius regarded the clash as a victory and to the men it was the first decent victory since they had arrived on the river especially, one supposes, Cornelius Scipio's army. Sempronius and Cornelius decided not to capitalise on this action, instead it was Hannibal who decided to initiate the battle. He scouted the area on the west bank of the Trebia and found a suitable hide for Mago and his cavalry to conceal themselves from any Roman force crossing the river. Hannibal decided to strike at dawn, as the Romans would only have sentries on duty, while the army was waking up and preparing for the day. He sent a small force of cavalry across the river to attack the camp and draw out the Romans while he had time to deploy his forces, ensuring that they were well prepared for battle. His cavalry quickly stirred up the Roman camp; Sempronius summoned the army to battle and sent his cavalry out after the retreating Carthaginian force. Hannibal had guessed right that the Romans would not miss a chance to attack his force again, as they seemed weak and as they knew the location of his camp they would come in force. The Roman cavalry crossed the river with ease and chased off the Carthaginian force, then probably saw the rest of Hannibal's army lined up ready for battle. Sempronius, on learning of this, brought out his army and rashly ordered them to cross the Trebia without any preparation. They were soaked when they emerged on the western bank in mid- December in northern Italy; Sempronius should have held fast on the eastern bank and instead waited for Hannibal to cross and hit him as he crossed.

Hannibal had already placed Mago and his cavalry in their hidden position and now he lined up his forces into a broad front. He placed his Gallic allies in the centre with his own heavy infantry on either side and on the flanks he placed his remaining cavalry with elephants, leaving his slingers in front to harass the Roman front line. Sempronius and Cornelius Scipio lined up their forces with the Velites in front facing the slingers, the four lines of Roman infantry and allied infantry in blocks with spaces between each unit and the cavalry guarding the flanks. Sempronius ordered the advance and the Roman heavy infantry, supported by the Velites, pushed aside the slingers. The Velites then move back into the main Roman body. The heavy infantry continued moving forward and hit the Gallic troops, forcing them back. At the same time Hannibal ordered the cavalry and elephants to hit the Roman cavalry; which quickly collapsed, were forced back and eventually off the battle field; therein leaving the infantry's flanks exposed. This meant that both consuls who fought in the cavalry were no longer commanding the Roman infantry. The Carthaginian cavalry, slingers and elephants now crashed into the exposed flanks of the infantry causing them to slow as they turned to fight them. This left the Roman centre moving forward and exposing its flanks to the Carthaginian heavy infantry.

At this point, with the Roman cavalry having retreated, Mago emerged from cover and charged in to the rear of the Roman and allied infantry, causing a collapse of the formation's rear. The Roman formations on the flanks and rear collapsed leaving only the centre, who continued to advance forward and broke through the Gallic infantry. This force remained intact, was able to leave the battlefield and according to the sources was about 10,000 strong, they retreated back to Placentia where they joined up with the remaining cavalry. Those forces that had been unable to escape were destroyed by Hannibal's forces. Some were forced to retreat into the river where they were cut down by cavalry and the Roman camp was taken and burnt. Hannibal, in his first proper battle with a twin consular army had proved himself the better tactician and had defeated four legions, their cavalry and allied support. The only good news for Rome was that it was now winter and Hannibal was unable to exploit his victory until the spring of 217 BC.

Scipio and Sempronius split their forces up; Sempronius spent the rest of the winter in Placentia and Scipio in Cremona. This left Hannibal controlling most of the Po valley and he now had access to the west coast of Italy, which meant he could march on Rome in the spring if he wanted to, as the two consuls had been forced to the east of the Po valley. Rome had suffered its first major defeat for a generation and its confidence in itself had been shaken; more importantly the confidence of its allies in Italy was also shaken. So far in the first year of the war, Rome had undertaken three offensives on three different fronts - Spain, Sicily / Carthage and defence of Italy. The campaign in Spain was a success; Sicily had been held, but the invasion of Carthage was called off due the direct threat from Hannibal, which Rome had not been unable to counter so far. Thus, Hannibal now had the initiative on the frontier of Italy.

At the start of 217 BC Sempronius arrived in Rome to oversee the election of the new consuls, who would take up their new posts on the ides of March 217 BC (15th of the month). Gnaeus Servilius and Gaius Flaminius were chosen. Sempronius now returned to Placentia. Hannibal was also busy during this period and, to keep his men occupied, he raided the region; picking off Roman colonies one at time. One such settlement was Vitumulae, who attempted to defend itself and was sacked. It may well be here that Hannibal began his policy of killing all able bodied Roman male citizens caught; according to Livy (1965). Whether this is propaganda and inserted here to emphasise the dire situation in Rome and its allies, is open to question.

In the spring Hannibal began his offensive by advancing first into Liguria; collecting local allies as he moved through the region, which allowed him to replace losses in his army. It also supported his claim that he was there to liberate the Italians from Roman oppression. Here again Livy (1965) emphasises this; the problem for us is whether this is hindsight by Livy to explain Hannibal's later actions, or a deliberate policy of Hannibal's.

Sempronius reacted to the advance of Hannibal by moving his forces to Luca (Lucca) to block any advance towards Pisae (Pisa) and a crossing point over the Arno River, which would then allow Hannibal to follow the coast to Rome. In Rome the threat of an attack by Hannibal caused consternation and the need again to consult the Sibylline prophecy books; which were consulted by the decemviri (a ten member college whose purpose was to interpret the prophecy and report back to the senate).

They decided, according to Livy (1965), that the city was unclean and so unworthy of the gods. They ordered that 9 days of supplication be undertaken by the entire city. The importance of omens and portents, (such as the timing of a flight of birds at dawn) could cause a whole day's proceeding in the city of Rome to be halted. A consul before battle would have a chicken, for example, killed and its insides examined to decide if today was the right day for the battle. So, shutting down the whole city for this period was not unusual as it was for religious reasons. The need to have gods with one was paramount to enable a successful outcome in public, as well as one's private life. So Rome was purified and meals were placed inside the temples of the gods; images of the gods placed on couches and food laid out as per fashion in Rome (stewing of the couches). Having the gods reside again in Rome would, they hoped, ensure victory against Hannibal[15].

In mid-March Flaminius was given command of Sempronius' army by the senate. According to Livy (1965) he rushed to meet Sempronius at Ariminum, which would mean Sempronius moving his troops half-way across the country and leaving Hannibal free to cross the Arno. Polybius (2010) does not mention this, or the controversy caused; according to Livy (1965) by not undertaking his religious duties and so causing the gods to curse him; Livy may well have introduced this to explain what happened next as it makes a good story. Servilius, as the remaining consul in Rome, would normally undertake these duties while his colleague was away, hence another reason for having two consuls. It is probable that Flaminius did go to Ariminum, not to meet Sempronius, but to meet the praetor Atilius and his two legions, then cross the Apennines and meet up in Etruria with Sempronius. In the meantime Servilius remained in Rome and raised the levy of men from Rome and their allies.

Flaminius met up with Sempronius at Arretium (Arezzo). Hannibal had not gone towards the coast but instead was moving inland, following the north bank of the spring flooded Arno; so Sempronius' forces were shadowing him from the south bank; Arretium lay on a southern bend in the

---

[15] Livy throughout his work always reports omens as they were considered warnings from the gods and needed to be dealt with

path of Arno. Hannibal, as he moved through Etruria, pillaged the land making examples of Roman citizens while sparing the locals; in an effort, as Livy states, to gain more allies in his campaign. Without doubt he pillaged, as his army needed food and any loot was just extra pay for them. Again Hannibal had the initiative as he could chose when to cross the river, the Roman forces had to wait for him to move; in the meantime Roman and allied property was being lost to Hannibal.

Lake Trasimene

Hannibal did cross into Umbria and he avoided Flaminius' army, bypassing them in Arretium and heading south towards Perusia (Perugia). Flaminius was now in a difficult position; Hannibal was now between him and Rome. He could summon his fellow consul, who had recruited his forces and crossed the Apennines to guard the east coast of Italy and await their arrival. But in the meantime Hannibal was advancing ever closer to Rome, so Flaminius took the obvious choice, summoned help from his fellow consul and set off after Hannibal hoping to catch him before he moved too far south. Hannibal quickly learnt of Flaminius' pursuit and located the prefect place in which to ambush his advancing column; the north eastern corner of Lake Trasimene. Here the road was caught between the foothills and lakeside, leaving very little room for the Romans to manoeuvre in. Hannibal had already learnt at the battle of the River Trebia how powerful the heavy Roman infantry was and its ability to manoeuvre and counter threats from not only the front, but its sides. So Hannibal decided to use this ability to his own advantage; the ambush position he choose would have the Roman army formed into a long column with gaps between each unit. So, when attacked they would turn to fight and so halt the column, allowing his men to pick off units when it was most advantageous, secondly communication between the front and rear of the column would be lost, so each unit would be isolated.

Hannibal, at this battle, would show his genius for picking the correct terrain to fight to his advantage, as well as the time and the correct tactics to use. All he needed to do was lure Flaminius into the trap. He had already gathered that Flaminius was under great pressure to succeed against him and so, he again used this to advantage; he slowed his advance down and waited in the ambush site for the arrival of Flaminius. Flaminius, after undertaking a forced march, reached the north western corner of the lake at sunset. Hannibal had some of his men set up camp at the far end of the northern shore and ensured that they made it as visible as possible, lighting lots of fires, in this way Hannibal hoped to convince Flaminius that he was unaware of his presence and so would be in camp next morning.

Flaminius fell into Hannibal's trap; he made camp and prepared to rush along the lake shore at dawn the next morning using the fog and mist to hide his advance on Hannibal's camp. Hannibal, during the night, had his men move into position overlooking the lakeshore and remain quiet not lighting fires etc... At dawn the Romans advanced along the lake shore, the scouts, if deployed, unless they had left the road and climbed into the foothills, would not have spotted the ambush. This was due to Hannibal also using the dawn mist and fog to hide his ambush, just as Flaminius had intended to do himself. As the front of the column approached Hannibal's camp, they saw part of his army deployed to block their advance. Flaminius at the front of the column probably ordered the advance, which may well have been the signal Hannibal was waiting for to spring the trap. As Hannibal planned; the Roman column was spread out along the lake shore and his men hit them from the foothills and from the rear; causing complete chaos in the column. The front of the column was unaware of what was happening and attacked the Carthaginians.

At some point Flaminius was killed, communications had already broken down. Only the front of the column was able to fight their way out and they escaped, only to be surrounded in a village the next day by Maharbal and his cavalry whom they surrendered to. The rest of the column was destroyed; in the end about 10,000 men were said to have managed to return from the ambush. Rome had now suffered its biggest defeat so far in the war to Hannibal; with four legions, their attached cavalry and allied troops destroyed. Sometime after the battle Servilius' advanced forces consisting of 4,000 cavalry, under G Centennius, arrived in the area to support the now destroyed army of Flaminius and they too ran into an ambush and were destroyed. The road to Rome was now open to Hannibal. Hannibal remained at the scene of the battle and collected the spoils which included Roman armour and weapons, with these he equipped his own Carthaginian infantry; converting from the old style phalanx to his version of the Roman phalanx.

Rome first learnt of the ambush and death of Flaminius several days later and this again caused chaos; to compound this came the news of the relief columns also defeated by Hannibal and the news that there was nothing to stop Hannibal at this time from advancing on Rome.

Fabius the Dictator

The senate met over the next couple of days to decide what to do next, probably in late spring. First they ordered a second draft of levies, not only from Rome, but from their allies; this would take time and mean the new army would be, at best, second rate as the best had already been chosen. Next they decided that the situation was so dire that a dictator needed to be appointed to wrest control of the situation and they elected the ex-consul and ex-dictator Quintus Fabius. They halted their business for the next six months while Fabius took control of the nation, his master of Horse (deputy) was Marcus Minucius Rufus and together they set about rebuilding Rome's defences and organising the city guard (a home guard, made up of those not considered suitable for the levy). Servilius retreated back towards Rome, leaving his army at Ocriculum (Otricoli), while he travelled into Rome to meet with Fabius. Rome had now been abandoned for the time being in the defence of eastern Italy.

Hannibal in the meantime had decided not to advance on Rome and crossed the Apennines. He attempted to take Spoletium (Spoleto) and then onto Picenum; Rome had now lost control of northern Italy and was steadily being boxed into the western side of Italy.

Fabius, following custom, had the sibylline books again consulted by the college of ten who ordered another period of cleansing of the city, as the last attempt had failed to appease the gods. Fabius delegated the majority of the rituals to the praetor Marcus Aemilius and he himself performed the major ceremony of dedicating a new shrine to Venus Erycina (in this guise the bringer of victory, as it had been taken from the Carthaginian city of Eryx during the last war). During this period Fabius also had his master of horse raise two legions and allied troops and arranged the levy to meet at the city of Tibur (Tivoli). Lastly, and perhaps, more damaging for Rome's allies, the city ordered all her citizens in un-walled settlements to retreat to walled towns and cities; and before leaving, to burn all crops and anything else that could be used by Hannibal's army.

Fabius was abandoning the countryside and Rome's main means of wealth production, as well as that of her allies. Following the Roman retreat from the north, a small Carthaginian raiding fleet attacked the port of Cosa; according to Livy (1965), while Polybius (2010) says it was Pisa. Fabius ordered Servilius to take part of the city guard to act as marines, as well as any warships in Rome or on the Tiber and defend the western coastline as the Carthaginians had also raided Corsica and Sardinia. Servilius returned order to Sardinia and Corsica and then spent the rest of the summer raiding the Carthaginian coastline from his new base of Lilybaeum on Sicily.

Probably in the early summer, Fabius moved Servilius' army from Ocriculum where they had been guarding the approaches to Rome from Hannibal, to Tibur where they linked up with the newly levied army. Now Fabius undertook his strategy of 'detached contact' with Hannibal; in an effort to deter Hannibal from attacking Rome he manoeuvred his army so that it blocked Hannibal's approach to Rome. In the process he avoided any major battles; instead concentrating on building up his new army. To keep them active, he sent them after any foraging party belonging to Hannibal. Hannibal in the meantime moved further south and into Greater Greece, looting any Roman colonies he came across. Both forces approached each other outside Arpi (an old Greek colony) in Apulia.

Fabius continued to shadow Hannibal as he moved along the Via Appia, crossing the Apennines to the Roman colony of Beneventum (Benevento) and then captured Telesia (Telese Terme); for the first time Hannibal threatened the major city of Capua; the capital of Campania. Instead he reached the coast at Sinuessa (Mondragone), a Latin city, and pillaged the area around the city. Fabius, on following, realised that Hannibal had trapped himself on the coast and set up a large ambush as part of a plan to bottle him in the region. He placed forces around Mt Callicula and Casilinum (modern Capua), a junction on the Via Appia and a major crossing on the River Volturnus. He recalled Minucius, who had been guarding the pass on the Via Appia at Tarracina, thus he blocked any advance north by Hannibal. Together they believed they had bottled up Hannibal and his forces; as the summer went on they would quickly run out of supplies and in this manner, they hoped to bring Hannibal to heel, without a fight.

The So-Called Battle of the Plain of Capua

Hannibal broke out of the trap by moving his forces at night. This was highly unusual. as it was fraught with danger and could easily lead to confusion and loss of forces in the darkness. So, to cover the movement and noise of his army as they broke out, he launched a very clever rouse using the looted cattle. He had grass and branches tied to their horns and then when these were set alight, they were driven at the Roman positions. The Romans, seeing the lights, assumed they were under attack and moved to fight what turned out to be the cattle. In the confusion the Romans abandoned the high ground and Hannibal's troops seized these positions, which allowed the column to move out of the plain. They may well have followed the river valley, reaching the safety of Allifae (Alife) at the base of the Apennines, a good distance from Casilinum. Placing them closer to Rome than Fabius.

Again Hannibal outwitted his Roman opponents and during the summer seemed to have led Fabius on a tour of Magna Graecia, whilst looting Roman property and smaller colonies. The result was that Rome still had a large army, but Hannibal was still free to pillage and was setting the pace, as well as keeping the initiative. But so far no major non-Roman town or city had joined Hannibal against Rome. His defeats of Romans in the north may have swayed the Gauls, but with a Roman army under Fabius still operating in the south, the allies were unlikely to change sides as Hannibal had yet to prove to them he could defeat Rome and then defend them.

The Battles of Gereonium

Hannibal then moved his forces to Gereonium in Apulia. Fabius moved his forces to Larinum (Larino), a short distance from Gereonium; from here he returned to Rome to deal with religious matters; according to Livy (1965) leaving the army under his deputy Minucius. Hannibal may well have been considering wintering in this area, but with Minucius now in charge, the deputy decided to take advantage of Hannibal being in camp and moved his camp closer, leaving only a hill and valleys between the two camps. Hannibal, by now well aware of the change of command, decided to test the 'metal' of the new commander and used his cavalry to taunt the Roman camp. Minucius reacted and a small skirmish developed with both sides suffering losses, but neither gaining any advantage from the fight.

News reached Rome and the story quickly developed into a victory. The people and senate led, according to Livy (1965), by the ex-praetor Gaius Terentius Varro, undermined the power of Fabius and the senate made the highly unusual action of granting joint dictator power to Minucius, according to Polybius (2010). Here Livy singles out Varro, referring to his plebeian background; how he was a rabble-rouser and was hated by the patrician class. This is difficult to accept as Varro had reached the magistrate rank of praetor; one below consul. This was a position he could not have reached without support and alliance of the patrician class. But Livy needed a tool, which Varro becomes, to explain Rome's continuing inability to defeat Hannibal and he clashes with Livy's and Polybius' hero of the moment Fabius.

Fabius, on returning to the Roman camp, split his command and Minucius removed his army and built a new camp close by. Hannibal again was aware of the change of command, probably from spies and deserters and saw another opportunity to lure the Romans out for a battle, thus releasing him from what was a safe winter camp and now an open prison. Fabius' tactics were already beginning to have the desired effect as Hannibal was relying more and more on the supplies he had already obtained, which would surely run dry during the winter. So Hannibal needed to lift the Roman blockade in order to survive the winter. First Hannibal deployed light infantry and cavalry into the valleys close to the hill and out of sight of the Roman positions. Then he deployed troops to the hill between the camps and set up a defence. Minucius sent out his Velites and cavalry to force Hannibal off the hill. Hannibal, waiting for this, moved his heavy infantry now equipped like the Romans, to counter this and they pushed the Velites and cavalry off the hill. Minucius was aware of this and sent his legions into the fray and pushed up the slope. Hannibal then deployed the hidden troops who attacked the Roman rear from the base of hill, catching the Romans again in a vice like ambush.

Fabius, now alerted to the developing battle, moved his forces to support Minucius and arrived on the scene just in time to stop the route of Minucius' army. The result was another draw, both armies remained in their position and Fabius now sat tight as autumn arrives; he and his forces had the surrounding region supplying them whilst Hannibal's foragers were continually under attack by Roman cavalry. So Hannibal faced an uncomfortable winter. In the late autumn Fabius and Minucius' power as dictators came to an end so they returned to Rome. Here, Livy (1965) becomes very confused by this and comes up with some wonderful story to explain how Rome copes with no consuls and no dictator until the New Year election of 216. It is not surprising, as he is writing in the period of Augustus the first emperor, the last dictator was Julius Caesar, who had been granted the dictatorship for life. So the republican government was not something he had any real knowledge of. Instead Polybius (2010) explains the situation better; Fabius returned to Rome to oversee the elections of the two new consuls to cover the gap between the end of his and Minucius powers as dictator and the ides of March; when the newly elected consuls would assume power. So Gnaeus Servilius Geminus and Marcus Atilius Regulus returned to power and replaced Fabius and Minucius as commanders of the armies encamped outside Hannibal's camp.

The senate continued to operate and did its best to make up for the lack of income due to Hannibal's assault on the countryside. They demanded any outstanding tribute from allies; Pineus of Illyria was one who had not yet paid and was ordered to do so, or hand over more royal hostages until he did. Hiero of Syracuse was also asked to assist; he sent a large amount of gold to help pay for the war, as well as 1,000 bowmen and slingers to make up for Rome's lack of these weapons, after-all it was now in his interest to see Rome defeat Carthage, as he was also an enemy of Carthage. It was also to show that Rome was still a major power. When they received word that their old enemy Philo had sought sanctuary at the court of Philip V of Macedon, they sent envoys demanding that Philip hand over this war criminal to them. Philip rejected this but Rome had made its point at least; it may be at war with Hannibal and Carthage, but it still remembered its enemies and wanted revenge.

The Spanish Campaign of 217

In the late spring of 217 Hasdrubal prepared for his summer campaign and assigned his enlarged fleet of 40 ships, according to Livy (1965), to Himilco. He advanced north from New Carthage with the army moving along the coast, the fleet shadowing and protecting him from any Roman fleet. Gnaeus Scipio, using similar tactics, advanced south from Tarraco. They come into contact at the mouth of the Ebro River. The Roman fleet attacked first and drove the Himilco's fleet onto the beach. The Roman fleet then managed to drag a number of undamaged ships off the beach and increased the size of their own fleet at a stroke. They then advanced along the Spanish coastline following the victory and sacked Onusa, before attacking the land around New Carthage. The fleet raided Longuntica capturing Himilco's naval supplies, before attempting to sack the island of Ebusus; part of the Balearic Islands. Following this, at some point during the summer, the Balearic Islands joined the Roman camp. The fleet returned to Tarraco for the winter. Gnaeus Scipio and his army moved inland from the coast behind Tarraco and defeated a large local tribe the Ilergetes, which encouraged more tribes to join the Roman side, as well as providing in-depth defence to the Roman conquests on the Spanish coastline north of the Ebro River.

They later revolted, but a small Roman force with allied support put down the revolt. Gnaeus Scipio returned in the late summer to Tarraco; where his brother Publius Scipio arrived with supplies and 2 legions. He probably had the rank of pro-consul, which gave him the 'imperium'; the power to command an army on behalf of the senate (only two consuls are allowed at one time, at the time the two consuls have resigned as Fabius holds the power of dictator, but he can't be everywhere, so Sempronius with the fleet may well have had pro-consular powers). The combined forces under Publius moved south and crossed the Ebro River to reach Saguntum and lay siege. Bostar the Carthaginian commander was persuaded, or duped, by a local chieftain called Abelux into handing over the Celtiberian tribal hostages to his keeping. Abelux already planned to join the Romans and give the hostages over to Publius, so securing his prominence in the Roman camp. Publius had the hostages sent home and so began to further undermine Carthaginian control of Spain.

So ended another successful year of campaigning in Spain by Rome.

Spring Italy 216 BC

In the New Year the elections for the consularship were held, according to Livy (1965); it was a most appalling spectacle, as Varro used his rabble-rousing skills and money to buy the consularship, which was normally how it was done. But Livy needed to blacken Varro even more as he prepared his readers for the events of 216 BC. So Varro and a former consul, Lucius Aemilius Paullus hero of the Illyrian campaign, were elected and assumed power on the 15th March 216 BC. Aemilius then appointed Servilius and Atilius as pro-consuls and they continued to command the armies surrounding Hannibal.

Aemilius began raising two more legions bringing the total number of Roman Legions in service to 8 in 216, as well as doubling the normal levy from Rome's allies. Four praetors were elected; Philus was given the task of running the city of Rome, Matho to judge cases between citizens and non-citizens (commercial and civil cases), Marcus Claudius Marcellus was given command of Sicily, and Lucius Potumius Albinus was sent with an army to Cisalpine Gaul to attack Hannibal's allies there.

The senate, in the summer, decided that the situation was so grave that the consuls were to combine forces and meet up with the pro-consuls. Hopefully with their combined army, they would be able to finally defeat Hannibal. Each consul took overall control of the army on alternative days. Both Polybius and Livy agree that neither consul liked each other and that both were intent on conducting the war differently. Paullus, with more experience, had decided to continue with the Fabian strategy of starving Hannibal into submission; Varro, a fresh consul, wanted a military victory as this would increase his standing, his wealth and his family's position in Rome and lastly be of great service to Rome. So Varro decided to take the initiative. The consular armies reached their camp sometime in late July and the difference in style became apparent, with Varro desperate to attack while Paulus was content to wait until Hannibal made a move.

Hannibal, by all accounts, was in a serious position; he had been unable to move from his winter camp at Gereonium and his foraging parties were continually under attack. Sooner or later he would have to break out of his winter camp, or risk losing everything. With the arrival of the new Roman army Hannibal decided to make his move. He could either launch a suicidal attack on the two fortified Roman camps or he could escape. He chose to escape, leaving his camp with the impression it was still occupied and moved his army at night; leaving everything they couldn't easily carry behind. Again the Roman's seemed unable to detect the rouse and he escaped the Roman noose. Moving through the hills he reached the town of Cannae, which was then the main Roman supply base. He also took the town and fed his army, camped outside the town on the northern bank of the river Aufidus. Paullus and Varro moved their army in pursuit and caught up with Hannibal on the plain to the northeast of the river. The pro-consular armies were placed on the northern side of the river facing Hannibal and the consular armies' camp was placed on the southern bank. The Romans had now blocked Hannibal from moving any further into Apulia, the other direction led, eventually, to Rome.

The Battle of Cannae 2nd August 216 BC

On the first day of August, Paullus was in control of the combined army and refused to move out of camp when Hannibal lined his forces up ready for battle. Hannibal had sent out his cavalry to attack the camps in an attempt to force the Romans to take to the field and open ground. Paullus had already decided that the flat plain offered Hannibal the tactical advantage, as this terrain was very suitable for his cavalry and was determined to hold his ground.

The next day it was Varro's turn and he decided to bring his forces out onto the plain; the pro-consular armies were mixed in with his. He placed his Roman cavalry under Paullus on his right flank next to the river, in the centre the legions and allied heavy infantry; not in standard formation but in close order, so that they presented a tighter formation and would be able to concentrate their power. The infantry were under the commands of the two pro-consuls; Servilius and Atilius. Varro then commanded the allied cavalry on the right wing. Hannibal brought his forces out and placed them in a similar formation to the one he used at the river Trebia, with one major change; the Gallic and Spanish infantry, instead of being in a straight line, were moved forward into a convex formation; pointing towards the Roman centre, on the end of each line he placed his Roman styled Carthaginian heavy infantry; under his and Mago's command. Opposite Paullus, he placed his Spanish and Gallic cavalry under Hasdrubal and against Varro he placed the Numidians under Hanno. The Roman Velites were placed in front of the Roman formation and the slingers and skirmishers of Hannibal lined up facing them.

Livy (1965) embellishes his account with lots of speeches by all the commanders involved in the battle. He comes up with an odd account, almost a little story that 500 Numidian cavalry deserted just before the battle and surrendered to the Romans. The Romans chose to accept them and place them under a light guard still on horseback behind their lines, something rather confusing. It is even more confusing as Polybius (2010) makes no mention of this incident whatsoever.

Hannibal's plan is much easier to understand once the battle is over; his plan was to allow the Roman heavy infantry, which he knew he couldn't stop head on, to advance into the Gallic and Spanish infantry, who would collapse under the pressure and pull back, thus collapsing the convex shape of their formation into a concave one. In the process the Roman infantry would rapidly advance past the Carthaginian infantry, who would then be able to turn inwards and hit the Roman infantry flanks. His cavalry's first task was to halt the Roman one from interfering in the battle and threatening his infantry, secondly if they drove off the Roman cavalry from each wing they would be free to swing around and as at Trebia; attack the Roman rear. What was unexpected was the tightness of the Roman infantry formation....

The Velites and Hannibal's skirmishers clashed; hurled projectiles into the others ranks and quickly returned to their own lines as the Gallic and Spanish cavalry charged into the Roman cavalry. These beings, due to the closeness of the river bank, were unable to manoeuvre and avoid a direct clash. Both cavalry quickly became stationary and dismounted in order to fight; Hannibal's slingers joined in and Paullus is thought to have been severely injured during the early part of the clash. Hasdrubal's forces began to push the Roman cavalry back towards the rear. Hanno launched his assault using space to surround and probe the allied cavalry. The effect was that for the remainder of the battle the Romans had lost their cavalry. The Spanish and Gallic infantry clashed head on with the advanced Roman infantry and as expected, they quickly fell back. As at the river Trebia; the Roman lead units quickly advanced, causing gaps to form in the formations behind them as they strove to catch up.

At some point the Roman infantry passed beside the Carthaginian heavy infantry and into the forming hollow in the centre of Hannibal's lines. When the moment was right, Hannibal ordered the heavy infantry to turn inward and attack the Roman flanks. This caused the Roman flanks to halt and deal with the new threat whilst the centre separated and continued forward; only to find itself also surrounded by the now, not so fleeing, Gallic and Spanish infantry. Hasdrubal completed his route of the Roman cavalry leaving Paullus dead. He moved his cavalry to the rear of the Roman lines causing the Roman allied cavalry to flee the battle with Varro in tow. Carthaginian cavalry units now descended on the Roman rear, causing even more chaos as the outer lines of the Roman formation were forced ever inward, crushing those in the centre. The result was that the Roman infantry and their allies suffered the heaviest casualties and were almost destroyed. Livy (1965) gives 40,000 Roman dead while Polybius (2010) gives almost twice that.

The result was that the only Roman army operating in Italy was completely destroyed by Hannibal. Dead on the battlefield was the Consul Paullus, the pro-consuls Atilius, Servilius and the recent dictator Marcus Minucius as well as the cream of the patrician class. The Roman survivors fled the battlefield and the figure of 4000 infantry and about 3700 cavalry made their way to Canusium (Canosa di Puglia), about 10 km southwest of the battle site. Gathered here was Varro, Lucius Metellus and four tribunes; one whom Livy (1965) tells us was Publius Cornelius Scipio. He goes on to build up the character of his saviour of Rome and eventual victor of the war, by having a young man rebuke his seniors for preparing to flee the country rather than stay and save it!

Chapter Four: The Second Punic War Part Two

The Aftermath of Cannae

Hannibal remained at the battle site while his men collected the spoils of war and enjoyed the victory. He made no effort to go after the survivors, who were less than half a day's march away. In some way it is not so surprising; his men had two Roman camps to loot, the enemy wounded to finish off and captives either to be sold as slaves, or to ransom. His men had only recently been on the point of starving and had been staring defeat in the eyes; Hannibal's army must have been drunk (literally) with the victory.

Hannibal had already failed to follow up at Lake Trasimene and move on to Rome and against Roman expectations he failed again to move on Rome. This time the city had little to defend it, after-all it was the middle of summer and if he laid a siege the city might not have been able to fill its granary's in time from the harvest. Even in Livy's time of writing, it still remained a mystery as to why Hannibal failed to follow up on such a huge victory. He has Maharbal rebuking Hannibal, BK XXII (51) (1965) in his text and finally fuming at him:

"No one has been blessed with all the gods' gifts. You know, Hannibal how to win a fight; you don't know how to use your victory".

In Livy's and many Roman's views at the time and later, it was that day and Hannibal's failure to attack, that saved Rome and its empire. Historians still argue about 'why' he did not move on Rome and in general there is argument to most assumptions on this topic for one solid reason; there is no Carthaginian account of the war and therefore no Carthaginian's idea on why he did not move. The consensus however, is that this was never Hannibal's plan. By following Livy, who inserted earlier in his account of the war the idea that Hannibal had only come to save the Italians from the Romans. In turn Livy can lead us to believe that he did not need to destroy Rome, instead by removing her allies he expected the city to surrender. But Marharbal's speech can also be seen as a rebuke of Hannibal's later campaign in southern Italy which lasted 13 years, in which he failed to defeat Rome and essentially wasted his time and energy, instead of confronting Rome head on when he had the clear advantage. Lastly, Hannibal was probably unaware of how Rome operated its economy and government. He may well have based his campaign on how Carthage would have survived cut off from its colonies, territories and trade; as Carthage was a net importer and so lacked resources to defend itself, hence its use of mercenaries. Rome however relied on its own population to supply troops and the area around it for food; so unless Rome was besieged she had access to resources and could therefore continue with the war.

In Rome news of the disaster was met with universal despair, the city appears to have gone into outright mourning; with the wives of the soldiers 'soaking the stones of Rome with their tears'. Livy (1965) is at his poetic best describing his vision of the scenes in Rome. The praetors summoned the senate to debate what to do next. Fabius recommended that the senate set an example and keep their wives out of sight, so as to encourage other fathers and brothers to keep the women from mourning in public, as this was further demoralising the city. He also suggested sealing the city and sending out scouts to learn what was happening in the countryside between Rome and Cannae.

The next decision by the senate was to elect a dictator; as far as they knew both consuls were dead and the city was leaderless. Marcus Junius was appointed; with Tiberius Sempronius Gracchus as his master of the horse. During the debate it was decided that Rome would not surrender, even if she didn't have an army in field at present. Livy doesn't say this but the actions that followed are that of a state unwilling to give up and digging in for the long haul. Junius ordered a fresh levy the second of the year and lowered the age limit to those under 17 and probably extended it to include those past the age limit. Next he ordered the release of debtors in exchange for military service and lastly, the most drastic of all actions, the state buying all male slaves suitable for military service from private citizens. He recruited, according to Livy, 4 legions and cavalry, as well as men from the Latin states. To pay for this the state borrowed from the gods. All this would take time so for the rest of August it seemed that Rome was defenceless. The next step was to recall Marcellus from Sicily with some of his forces and ships to protect the coast from any potential invasion from Carthage; Hiero of Syracuse was left to defend himself.

Then Junius dealt with the spiritual problems; Rome had suffered the second biggest defeat, even though she acted as the Sibylline books instructed. So Quintus Fabius Pictor[16] was sent to Delphi to seek guidance from Apollo. Word reached Rome soon after the defeat that Varro and a small part of the army had gathered at Canusium. Also the casualty list reached the city where the senate, now knowing the true extent of defeat, had 30 days of mourning set aside for the city to deal with their losses. Varro was ordered to return to the city; Livy (1965) thought that instead of him being welcomed as a hero, he should have been treated as the Carthaginians did to a defeated general; crucified as an example to others. Marcellus was given command of what wass left at Canusium, this was followed by news that most of Apulia and Samnium had gone over to Hannibal's side. Rome had not only been defeated by Hannibal, but worse her allies had betrayed her. Hannibal was just an enemy, the allies had in Rome's direst hour betrayed her, and she would not forget those actions.

In the meantime, Hannibal began to extend his control of Italy, Carthalo was sent to Rome with a delegation of leading Roman prisoners; the main mission was to establish the terms of Rome's surrender, while the prisoners were there to plead for their return, in exchange for a large payment to Hannibal. Junius refused to allow Carthalo to enter the city, sending back the message that Rome was still at war with them. It is likely that he refused to allow the prisoners to enter Rome too, as their presence would cause another drop in morale. Livy (1965) gives an alternate account but the result is the same; Rome didn't want its cowards returned, instead they were rebuked for not standing firm and dying where they stood.

Mago was then given the task of controlling the newly allied towns and cities in Apulia and Samnium. At some point following the victory at Cannae, Hannibal sent Mago to Carthage. Mago spoke to the senate/council in Carthage and presented them with a token of victory; all the gold rings removed from the dead of the battle. He then requested supplies and men, Carthage sent Hannibal more Numidian cavalry, elephants and silver so he could continue with the war. Mago was then sent to Spain with a large amount of silver to recruit and train a new army, and then bring it to Hannibal in Italy.

Hannibal's control extended; as most of the old southern Greek colonies went over to him, such as Tarentum (Taranto), Metapontum (Bernalda), Crotone and Locris (Locri); giving Hannibal access to ports in the Adriatic Sea and Ionian Sea. He then advanced into Campania; his real need was for a

---

[16] One of Rome's first historians, one of the main sources for Polybius (who critiques him) and Livy, his work has not survived.

port in the Tyrrhenian Sea so that Carthage could supply him directly with less chance of Rome intercepting the trade, either by sea or by land as had occurred before. His first attempt was at Neapolis (Naples), but it refused to surrender and Hannibal moved to Capua, which surrendered to him without a fight. Hannibal now controlled a city in Campania with access to the sea. The effect of this defection on Rome was so great that Livy (1965), writing less than 200 years after the event, was still fuming over the treacherous act of Capua against Rome in his works.

Rome goes on the Offensive

In September Marcellus had reached Casilinum and was ordered to defend Nola (north east of Mt Vesuvius) from Hannibal. He marched along the Appian Way through Calatia, reaching the city before Hannibal, and proceeded to mount a strong defence. Rome also dispatched the prefect Silanus to assist Neapolis in its defence. Hannibal retreated and then moved on to Nuceria (Nocera Inferiore), which he stormed and sacked. Hannibal then returned to Nola and began to besiege the town with his army. Marcellus divided up his army into three formations, one under Flaccus, the second under Aurelius and the remainder under himself. He placed each one at the gates closet to Hannibal's besieging army. Marcellus had Flaccus and Aurelius place their troops outside the gates, while he kept his behind the gate closest to Hannibal. In the late afternoon he ordered Flaccus and Aurelius to assault Hannibal's army.

Hannibal reacted as Marcellus expected and his army turned to face the attack on their flanks. At this point Marcellus, with his troops, storms out through the gate catching Hannibal's troops in the flanks. Marcellus wins the battle and Hannibal had now failed twice to take Nola. Hannibal retreated back to Acerrae (Acerra), half-way between Nola and Neapolis, and sacked it. Marcellus then moved his forces to Suessula, placing himself between Hannibal and Capua. Hannibal then moved on Casilinum and attempted to take the town, but the defenders, made up from the delayed levy from Praeneste (Palestrina) under Marcus Amicius, held out. The master of the horse, Tiberius Sempronius, moved to support the garrison but was not allowed to directly attack Hannibal for fear of losing any more troops. Marcellus however was unable to offer support as the River Volturnus had flooded its plain. Hannibal, now unable to take the city, left a small force to keep the defenders bottled up and he retired with the rest of the army to Capua for the winter. The town of Petelia, the last remaining Roman ally in Bruttian, begged for Roman support but the senate was unable to send any forces to assist and had to admit that they would just have to defend themselves; as all resources were now being used to hold Campania. So Petelia was left to fend for itself.

The situation was so serious in Rome that she was unable to send supplies to Sicily and Sardinia. In Sicily, Marcellus' deputy Otacilius was forced to beg for food and money from Hiero. Hiero also supported the Roman fleet under the praetor Publius Furius, but also suffered from the fallout from Cannae, as his eldest son Gelo attempted to mount a coup with support from an anti-Roman faction in the city of Syracuse. This failed and Gelo was executed. The situation was similar in Sardinia where the pro-praetor Cornelius Mammula was forced to take supplies from the local population to keep his army going.

In the late autumn the senate was very short of members and now had to elect the new consuls and praetors. The normal procedure, interrupted by the severity of the situation however, would be for the senate to have elected a censor to select suitable candidates to join their ranks. As the current dictator was unable to return himself as he was needed with his army, the senate either elected a temporary censor or another dictator, Marcus Fabius Buteo. He quickly choose the new batch of replacement senators; Livy (1965) gives the number as 170 and all had to have obtained the magistrate rank of Aedile, but once this was done Buteo resigned. In December Junius and Tiberius Sempronius, his master of horse, along with Marcellus arrived in Rome to oversee the elections of the new consuls and praetors. Tiberius Sempronius Gracchus was elected consul along with the Praetor Lucius Potumius Albinus who was still in Cisalpine Gaul. He was ordered to return to Rome in time to take up his consularship.

At the end of the year Rome had one army in Spain under the Scipio brothers, one in Cisalpine Gaul under Potumius and three surrounding Rome under Varro, Marcellus and the dictator Junius. The dictatorship of Junius was due to end in the January of 215, thus he remained near the capital. The town of Petelia though remained under siege for several months by Himilco, surrendering only after it ran out of food; the town knew that no Roman army would ever come to its aid whilst it remained on guard. Luckily for Rome the port and city of Rhegium stayed loyal to them.

Spain 216

Publius Scipio took command of the land forces and his brother Gnaeus took command of the fleet. Hasdrubal received reinforcements from Carthage and orders to march into Italy to support Hannibal. In the spring before he could leave, a local tribe called the Tartesii under Chalbus revolted and took the town of Ascua, tying Hasdrubal down and upsetting his plans to leave. He sent a message to Carthage informing them of the situation and in response they sent Himilco with more troops and ships to take control of Spain during his absence. In the meantime other Iberian tribes joined the revolt and Hasdrubal was forced to suppress them. At that time the Scipio brothers crossed the Ebro River and attacked Ibera close to the river. They failed to take it, but forced Hasdrubal to suspend his campaign and to move towards halting the Roman invasion. If this was the Scipio brothers' plan, it had the effect of giving the tribes a breather.

Both forces met close to Ibera; Hasdrubal formed his army into the normal Carthaginian formation. He placed his Spanish troops in the centre, on his left the Libyan troops; these were supported by his allied cavalry, on his right the Spanish were supported by Carthaginian infantry and Numidian cavalry. The Scipio brothers adopted the standard Roman formation; with the Velites at the front, the heavy infantry (unlike at Cannae) in open order with the cavalry on either flank. The Roman heavy infantry swept into the Spanish centre and it collapsed, unlike Cannae they were not in a convex formation to stand it, so they fell quickly behind the Carthaginian heavy infantry on either side. The Romans were struck on either front by this infantry but unlike at Cannae they were not in a three-sided trap. The centre, still advancing at that time, split as they passed the Carthaginian heavy infantry and swept into their flanks. The cavalry on either side clashed but played no further part in the battle. The Roman infantry destroyed their opponents and Hasdrubal fled the battlefield leaving his camp for the Romans to sack. Hasdrubal abandoned his plans to support Hannibal and retired back to New Carthage. The Scipio brothers also retired back across the Ebro River.

So at the end of 216, the Romans had defeated a Carthaginian army but not extended their control in Spain. They had also blocked Hasdrubal from supporting his brother in Italy, again showing how important the decision by Publius to send his brother into Spain was.

Spring Italy 215

In the spring Hannibal returned to Casilinum and lay siege, the garrison surrendered quickly as it had run out of food, Hannibal released them on payment of a ransom and they returned to Cumae. Casilinum was now in Hannibal's hands and he left a garrison behind to hold the town securely.

Rome's overall strategy for the year appears to have been to contain Hannibal in southern Italy and stop him linking up with the Gauls in Cisalpine Gaul, and thereby opening up a two-front campaign against Rome. In spring Rome received the news that the Praetor Lucius Potumius Albinus and his troops had also been destroyed in Cisalpine Gaul. The senate now had to wait for the right auspices to elect a new consul. According to Livy (1965) the senate first elected Marcellus as the new consul, but a clap of thunder as he went to take his position caused him to believe the gods were against him, and so he resigned; the senate then elected Fabius as consul.

The two regular legions in Sicily were ordered back to Rome and were placed under the command of the praetor Valerius; part of Marcellus' force was made up of the survivors of Cannae[17] and were sent to replace them in Sicily under the praetor Appius Claudius. The consul Gracchus took over the army made up predominately of slaves and Varro was also given pro-consular power. Fabius then recruited a new army and arranged for them to assemble at Sinuessa along with Junius' army. Marcellus returned to Nola. Fabius ordered all farmers to collect their grain and move it inside walled cities or towns to ensure that Hannibal was not able to obtain any extra supplies, secondly it ensured that Rome had secured supplies for the summer and in case of a siege. The praetor Valerius was ordered to take his legions to Apulia and take over the defence of the region, while Varro and his forces were directed to move by ship and set up defences around Tarentum. Before leaving he was ordered to recruit more troops from Rome's allies in Picenum. The Adriatic fleet was then based at Tarentum to defend the coast between the port and Brundisium (Brindisi). The city prefect Fulvius was also given ships with which to defend the Tiber. Finally Titus Crassus, after completing his assigned temple duties, was sent to Sicily with pro-consular powers to command the fleet.

In the spring Mago reached Spain with his newly recruited army and a fleet, along with orders for Hasdrubal to invade Sardinia. Hannibal also made an alliance with Philip V of Macedon, potentially opening up a new front against Rome. Philip agreed to invade the east coast of Italy and following the defeat of Rome, Hannibal agreed to attack Philip's Greek enemies. Rome learnt of this alliance after Philip and Hannibal's representatives were intercepted at sea.

The ill prefect of Sardinia was replaced by the praetor Titus Manlius Torquatus as news arrived in Rome that some of the Sardinian tribes led by Hampsicora revolted and so Manlius brought reinforcements along with him. Manlius then began to suppress the revolt, when news arrived that Hasdrubal the Bald, with a fleet after first being waylaid by a storm, had landed on the island. Manlius withdrew his forces back to the port of Carales (Cagliari). Hasdrubal joined up with Hampsicora and they moved on Carales. Outside the port the Roman and joint Carthaginian/Sardinian forces clashed and Manlius defeated them. He captured Hasdrubal the Bald, Hanno and a Mago. The survivors of the battle fled to Cornus; Manlius besieged it and took it, ending the Carthaginian invasion and Sardinian revolt. The Roman fleet under Titus Otacilius, operating out of

---

[17] As they were in disgrace they were sentenced by the senate to serve outside of Rome for the duration of the war

Lilybaeum, after raiding the area around Carthage had run into Hasdrubal the Bald's fleet as it made its way to Carthage and scattered it. At the end of the summer Manlius returned with his forces and prisoners to Rome.

Gracchus spent the late spring training his new army and moving them from Sinuessa to Iternum. Following a request for assistance from Cumae, as it was under siege from a Campanian army, he moved his forces to the city. He reached the city and during the first night there, he undertook a night attack on the enemy camp at Hamae and swiftly destroyed it. Hannibal, now aware of the consul's army's move towards Cumae, lay siege to the city, but Gracchus defended it well and Hannibal called off the assault.

Tiberius Sempronius, now commanding a force, defeated Hanno near Grumentum (Grumento Nova), forcing him to retire from Lucania (province of Basilicata) back to Brutlium (Calabria). Sempronius then secured the "toe" of Italy and so protected Sicily from Hannibal. Valerius retook Vercellium, Viscellium and Sicilinum (southern tip of the Apennines), and executed the town leaders for treason; then he retired back to Luceria (Lucera). Fabius campaigned during the summer and captured Compulteria (Alvignano), Trebula (Treglia) and Austicula along with their Carthaginian garrisons in the process. From there he moved his army to block Hannibal's camp at Tifata (Mt Tifata) from Capua. Marcellus remained in Nola over the summer.

Bomiclar arrived at Locri with more reinforcements from Carthage and marched to Bruttium to join up with Hanno. Hannibal, in the summer, now moved against Nola, Hanno marched north with his reinforced army and joined him at Nola; they both began their siege of the town. Marcellus again struck out from the town and attacked the besiegers, breaking the siege. During the siege a small number of Numidian and Spanish cavalry defected from Hannibal's army and joined Marcellus. Both Hannibal and Hanno withdrew from Nola; Hannibal then marched to Arpi for the winter. Hanno however, returned to Bruttium. From Bruttium he besieged Locri which, after the Roman garrison escaped by sea, surrendered and Hamiclar occupied the city. The Bruttians, under Hanno's directions, then began to besiege Croton which quickly fell; however, the elite of the town were allowed to find sanctuary at Locri.

Fabius was aware that Hannibal was at Nola and moved his forces close to Capua and disrupted their harvest; forcing the city to defend its fields. He remained outside Capua into the autumn, collecting up fodder from their fields and taking it back with him as he retired for the winter at Suessula. In the late autumn he ordered Marcellus to dismiss most of his army as Nola could not support them for another winter and Marcellus sent those men back to Rome. Gracchus remained at Luceria for the winter and Valerius stayed at Brundisium.

Overall Rome had been able to slowly regain a small number of towns, lost Croton and Locri and defended Nola successfully for a third time. They had held Sardinia and kept Hannibal in the south of Italy. Most importantly she had not suffered a military defeat, instead she had been victorious. But for Rome the real shock was how quick the southern Italians were to take up arms against them and support Hannibal.

Sicily 215

Hiero of Syracuse, Rome's vital ally in Sicily died, probably, in the early half of the year. His fifteen-year-old grandson was to inherit, but, still being a minor, he was placed under the guardianship of Adranodorus (uncle-in-law), Zoippus (uncle-in-law) and Thraso. Adranodorus and

Zoippus hatched a plot a in which Thraso was implicated and thus executed for treason. Zoippus was then sent on a mission to Egypt, while Adranodorus put into action the real plot and murdered his nephew while visiting Leontini (Lentini). He returned to Syracuse and he seized control of the city. Quickly he switched from being Rome's ally to that of Hannibal's. Claudius sent envoys to the city seeking confirmation of the change of sides and they confirm Adranodorus' change. Claudius then swiftly moved Roman forces to the borders of Syracuse and informed the senate. The Roman fleet was then sent to blockade Syracuse in an effort to stop Carthage or Hannibal sending any form of support. Rome now had an extra front to deal with, one where it had been expected least.

Spain 215

Due to the lack of supplies and money from Rome, the Scipio brothers began to exploit the region of Spain that they held and used it to pay for the army and navy. Rome was aware of the situation and developed a novel method to pay for the Spanish campaign; they put it out to private tender. The wealthy of Rome were encouraged to invest in supporting the campaign and contracts were agreed with a number of these; in exchange for non-conscription they paid for the supplies and cash to pay for the army. The state also agreed to cover any losses to shipping. They were to be repaid in full at the end of the war. The result was that the Scipio's received all the supplies and cash they needed during the summer.

During this summer Hasdrubal launched an assault on one of Rome's newest allies based at Iliturgi (Mengibar). The Scipio brothers moved their army to support the allies and defeated Hasdrubal's army forcing him to retire from the town. Later Hasdrubal moved against Intibili and again the Scipio's broke the siege and forced Hasdrubal to retire for the winter. More Iberian tribes moved to the Roman side following the Scipio's support of their allies. For Rome the campaign season in Spain had not gained any new territory, but they had once again defeated Hasdrubal in battle and slowly gained more allies.

Spring Italy 214 BC

Fabius returned to Rome and oversaw the election of the new consuls and praetors. Fabius was re-elected consul and Marcellus[18] was also elected consul. Flaccus also returned for a second time as praetor, Fabius' son Quintus Fabius was elected praetor, as well as Titus Crassus and Publius Cornelius Lentulus. Fabius and the senate again agreed that the pro-consuls and ex-consuls, praetors and pro-praetors should continue with their commands. The Romans had clearly learnt that continuity of command would be a key to defeating Hannibal. The next decision was to bring the Roman army up to a total of 18 legions.

Commander	Number of Legions	Region
Gracchus (pro-consul)	2 Slave/ debtor	Luceria
Fabius (Consul)	2 new legions	Rome (during election of the censors)
Marcellus (Consul)	2 new legions	Nola
Varro (pro-consul)	1	Picenum
Marcus Valerius (pro-praetor)	1 (marines)	Brundisium
Quintus Mucius	2	Sardinia
Praetor Fabius	2	Apulia
Pomponius	2	Cisalpine Gaul
City Prefect	2	Rome
Publius Cornelius Lentulus	2	Sicily

The fleet was also brought up to a total of 150 ships, with Titus Octacilius commanding the main fleet at Lilybaeum. The continuing cash crisis caused the senate and the consuls to take an unusual step; following on from the private financing of the war in Spain they now needed the same done to pay for the increased size of the fleet. For the first time the lower middle class were taxed in kind; they had to supply one sailor and 6 months wages. The wealthiest of the middle class was to supply three sailors and one year of wages and the patrician class, the wealthiest, was to supply eight sailors and one year's pay. With this in place Rome was able to build up her fleet.

There was also a lack of silver in the treasury, so the army was now paid in credit notes, redeemable at the end of the war for their value in silver coins. Widows and veterans were also paid in this manner, saving the state from going bust. Livy (1965) remarks that it became patriotic in Rome to be seen accepting these notes in lieu of cash.

In the spring Hannibal was still in need of a port on the western side of Italy; so by moving from Arpi to his old camp at Tifata, he then began a campaign from the camp, first moving up to the Lake of Avernus (Lago d'Averno) (after making an offering to his gods) and he moved to Puteoli (Pozzuoli). Fabius, on learning of the move by Hannibal, summoned Gracchus to take his forces to

---

[18] Although this is the first year he serves a consul, it is counted as his second term as a consul, see Spring 215

Beneventum, while the praetor Fabius relived him in Luceria. Hannibal retired on learning of the movement of Fabius and Gracchus and moved back to the outskirts of Naples where he burnt the fields, and then returned to Nola.

Marcellus, after forming up his new army at Cales (Calvi Risorta), marched them swiftly to Suessula. Once in camp he sent a legion back to Nola to stiffen its defence.

Fabius now planned to retake Casilinum; Hanno marched northwards but failed to reach Beneventum before Gracchus. On learning that Hanno was close by, he left the town and sought battle with Hanno. Hanno was beaten on the battlefield and abandoned his camp to the Romans. As a reward for his army defeating Hanno he was granted the freedoms of, with the permission of the consuls, the slaves in his army.

Marcellus now moved his army nearby to where Hannibal had camped, close to Nola. He attempted to place a unit of cavalry behind Hannibal during the night, but they became lost in the dark and failed to reach the intended position. The next day Marcellus moved to fight Hannibal who came out of camp for battle. Marcellus defeated him on the battlefield and Hannibal retired to his camp. Two days later, Hannibal broke camp after failing to besiege Nola and headed towards Tarentum.

In Rome two censors were elected and one of the tasks they dealt with was Cannae and those officers who, under Metellus, had planned to leave Italy. They were punished by being stripped of their rank and placed in the lowest level of society; the *aeraii*, along with those who had dodged the levy. The senate, to further punish the levy dodgers, conscripted them as ordinary soldiers, and along with those who survived Cannae, they were to serve for the duration of the war and sent to join those men in Sicily.

Fabius was now able to lay siege to Casilinum and with Hannibal moving away from Nola, ordered Marcellus to join him. The first attack failed, but the town quickly surrendered after Marcellus' troops seized one of the gates.

Gracchus dispatched some of his cavalry to raid enemy farms in the region; they ran into Hanno's main force and were almost wiped out.

Marcellus, following the capture of Casilinum, returned to Nola and Fabius to the Samnium region where he retook the towns of Compsa (Conza della Campania), Fugifulae, Orbitanium, Blandae in Lucania and Aecae (Troia) in Apulia. The praetor Fabius also retook Acuca and built a new camp at Ardoneae (Ordona). Hannibal failed to reach Tarentum in time to take the port, as Valerius had already dispatched a garrison to hold the port under Marcus Livius. From there Hannibal retired to winter at Salapia (Salpi).

For Rome the campaign season for 214 had been a success, they had again contained Hannibal in southern Italy and not lost a major engagement to him. The army, as a whole, was developing confidence and skills with the continual success their commanders had given them. Hannibal again had failed to achieve any major success against Rome; he had failed again to take Nola and had been unable to break out of southern Italy - he was now beginning to loose support.

Sicily 214

In the spring, Adranodorus himself was assassinated under orders of the council of Syracuse for his part in killing Hieronymus. This was followed by the murder of Adranodorus' and Zoippus' families. The city elected Hippocrates and Epicycdes, the envoys from Hannibal, as the new city magistrates, confirming that Syracuse was in league with Hannibal and Carthage. Hippocrates led Syracuse forces to Leontini and then raided the surrounding Roman property. In the late summer the senate ordered Marcellus to move his forces to Sicily and on his arrival, jointly with Appian, they seized Leontini. Hippocrates fled with his remaining troops to Herbesus, where he was joined by Epicycdes who reported that the council of Syracuse had exiled them. They marched on Syracuse, where they were met by the army which was meant to stop them but, instead, joined them. The pair entered the city, with the assistance of the general population, and had their enemies in the council killed. The people elected the pair as their generals and they rejected Marcellus' attempts to bring the city back into alliance with Rome.

Marcellus laid siege to the city, which was surrounded by walls from coast to coast, also with a fortified harbour.

Within the city lived Archimedes, who Livy (1965) says prepared all the engines of defence for Syracuse; from the position and type of artillery to putting protected shooting holes in the city's many walls. Marcellus launched a combined land and sea attack; the land attack failed due to the intense artillery fire from the walls. The sea attack was more complicated as Marcellus' engineers lashed two warships together to support siege towers. These were supported by each warship's marines giving covering fire. The assault failed as Archimedes had devised a number of cranes with grappling hooks sited on the walls. As Marcellus' ships had approached the walls, the grapples were lowered and hooked onto the bow of a ship, for example; using a system of counter weights the crane had proceeded to lift the bow of the ship, out of the water. It then released it, dropping the ship back so rapidly into the harbour that it sank.

Marcellus resorted to a prolonged siege, placing camps along the perimeter of the city's walls (probably closer to gates) and the fleet was tasked with blockading the port. The siege would last as long as the city had supplies, or until Marcellus' forces broke into the city, or a relieving force broke the siege.

Marcellus sent part of his army into the hinterland and retook Helorus (Noto)[19] and Herbesus without a fight, while he successfully stormed into Megara (Augusta).

Carthage was not sitting idly by as its old enemy suddenly changed sides. It dispatched Himilco with a large force to the island, they landed and seized Heracla (Capobianco di Cattolica Eraclea) and then took the city of Agrigentum (Agrigento). Carthage and Hannibal had returned to the island and begun to retake all the towns and cities they lost to Rome during and after the First Punic war; honour was restored both to Carthage and to Hannibal's family (e.g. Hamiclar). Bomiclar, commanding the fleet, then broke the blockade of Syracuse and brought his fleet into port. He pulled out shortly afterwards, not wishing to be caught inside the harbour when the Roman fleet turned up in force. Hippocrates, with the news of a Carthaginian invasion, broke out of the city with a large force and moved to join Himilco, leaving Epicycdes in charge. Marcellus had already sent part of his army towards Himilco, leaving a gap that Hippocrates noticed and used. Marcellus, in danger of being caught between two armies, turned around and caught Hippocrates still building his evening camp at Acrillae (Chiaramonte Gulfi).

A short battle ensued with Marcellus rounding up the Syracusian infantry while Hippocrates and his cavalry escaped to Acrae (Palazzolo Acreide). There he was joined by Himilco who was marching along the Via Selinuntina which ran from Gela to Syracuse (Chowaniec, 2012). Roman forces were

---

[19] Source for the modern place names in Sicily (Sciarretta, 2002)

also landed at Panormus (Palermo), they marched along the north side of the island to avoid Himilco and reached Marcellus' main camp outside Syracuse. Himilco moved inland and took Murgantia (close to Aidone). The Roman garrison of Henna (Enna), fearing the population was going over to Syracuse, massacred the town's population. Livy (1965) suspected that the commander of the garrison was not punished as it served as a warning to other Sicilian towns thinking of changing sides.

By the winter of 214, Hippocrates had based himself at Murgantia and Himilco at Agrigentum. Marcellus rebuilt the defences of Leontini and it became the main Roman supply base for his army surrounding Syracuse. Appius Claudius, who had remained at the siege camps, returned to Rome to be elected consul. He was replaced by Titus Crispinus who took over the camp and the fleet. Rome had begun the year in Sicily minus one ally, and at the end of the year, there were now three enemy armies facing Rome ready to fight for the control of island and Rome had already lost one port. Sicily, rather than Southern Italy, was now the most dangerous threat facing Rome; loss of the island would cripple the Roman economy and would potentially lose them the war, just as the loss of the island lost Carthage the First Punic War. Carthage, for the first time in two years had something to celebrate; she had regained Agrigentum and had a foothold in Sicily.

Greece 214

Finally, as the senate expected, Philip V of Macedon made his move against Rome. He attempted to storm Apollonia (Pojan in Albania) taking Oricum (Butrint[20]) opposite the island of Corfu as he moved along the coast to the city. Marcus Laevinus based at Brundisium, on receiving the report from Oricum and Apollonia, moved most of his army by ship under the command of Quintus Crista, landed at Oricum and retook the city. He then moved on Apollonia, relieved the city and destroyed the siege camp of Philip V; forcing him to flee inland and retreat back in tatters to Macedon. Rome had now deterred a major new threat to the east of Italy and again began campaigning in Illyria. For a country almost on the verge of defeat two years before, she had now launched a fresh campaign and the potential to enlarge the Roman Empire.

Spain 214

The Scipio brothers opened the campaign season by crossing the Ebro river to Castulo[21] (close to Linares) to support the Iberian tribes who were under increasing military pressure from Hasdrubal Barca. Hasdrubal moved from Castulo (which appears to have gone over to the Roman side) to Iliturgi where Gnaeus Scipio, commanding part of the army, broke Hasdrubal's siege of the town. Hasdrubal then moved on to besiege Bigerra (Bejar), possibly Livy, (1965) is mistaken here as the city lies in Salamanca, western Spain), which is where Gnaeus again breaks the siege. Once more Livy cites Munda (La Lantejuela) as the site of a battle between Gnaeus (who was wounded) and

---

[20] Part of a collection of Albanian national parks see http://www.butrint.org/index.php (accessed August 2012)

[21] According to Livy the home town of Hannibal's wife

Hasdrubal, and again he may well be mistaken, as this was the site of a battle during the Roman civil war and is close to Gades.

Finally, close to the end of the season, both armies clashed at Aurinx (Jaen) (again Livy may well be mistaken in the location) due west and well inland of New Carthage. Here again, Gnaeus was successful. If Livy is correct with his place names, then the Scipio brothers at this point in the war had cut New Carthage and the coastline off from the hinterland and the Iberians tribes, as well as threatening the silver mines. At the close of the season the Scipio brothers captured the city of Saguntum. Again Spain was the success for Rome and the campaign season for 214 had presented Hasdrubal with no major victories, let alone containing Rome above the Ebro River.

Italy 213 BC

In the New Year the consul and praetor elections were held, Quintus Fabius (son of Fabius) and Tiberius Sempronius Gracchus were elected consuls with Publius Sempronius Tuditanus, Gnaeus Fulvius Centumalus, Marcus Atilius and Marcus Aemilius Lepidus elected praetors.

Commander	Number of legions	Location for 213	Last commander
Q Fabius	2	Apulia	Fabius
Gracchus	2 slave/ debtor	Lucania	Gracchus
Aemilius	2	Luceria	
Tuditanus	2	Ariminum	Pomponius
Centumalus	2	Suessula	
Marcellus pro-consul	2	Syracuse	Marcellus
Lentulus pro-praetor	2	Sicily	Lentulus
Octacilius	Fleet	Sicily	Octacilius
Marcus Valerius pro-praetor	2	Greece and Illyria	Valerius
Quintus Mucius	2	Sardinia	Mucius
Varro pro-consul	1	Picenum	Varro

Both consuls were ordered to operate directly against Hannibal, 2 new legions and 20,000 allied troops were levied. Fabius became a commander under his son, the consul Q. Fabius, and moved against Arpi. It surrendered, Spanish troops opted instead to serve under him, the remainder were sent to Hannibal and Q Fabius left behind a garrison. Gracchus then took Atrinum. Hannibal spent the summer in the area of Tarentum; Calabrian towns now without protection came over to his side. In Bruttium; Consentia (Cosenza) and Taurianum (Palmi) returned to the Roman side. Hanno caught a Roman raiding force in the region and severely defeated them. Gracchus maintained control of Lucania. Livy (1965) has very little to say concerning the campaign in Italy for this year.

Hannibal had again failed to make any progress in the south; he gained a number of towns in one part and then, in another, the towns went back to Rome. For Rome there were no major defeats and Hannibal was still contained in the south; the longer he remained there the stronger Rome's forces were becoming, and the more confident. Both consuls were unable to return to Rome in the winter for the new consular elections (something must have been happening which Livy has failed to report, or lacked sources for); instead they choose Gaius Centho to act as dictator with Quintus Flaccus acting as his master of horse. They held the elections and Quintus Flaccus and Appius Claudius were elected consuls, with Gnaeus Fulvius Flaccus, Gaius Nero, Marcus Silanus and Publius Cornelius Sulla elected praetors. The dictator and his master of horse resigned following the election. One Publius Cornelius Scipio was elected Aedile according to Livy (1965) at the age of 23, instead of having to wait until he was at least 36 years; it showed the power and wealth of the Scipio family in Rome at this time.

Spain 213

In Spain the Scipio brothers were not only active militarily but diplomatically as well. They made contact with Syphax; a prince of one of the major Numidian tribes and persuaded him to join them and revolt against Carthage. Carthage reacted by arming a rival Numidian prince; Gala and his son Masinissa. With Carthaginian military support they drove Syphax into modern northern Morocco. Syphax recruited a new army and Masinissa, with Numidian cavalry, pursued the civil war into Morocco. The Scipio brothers developed their alliances with the Iberian tribes, recruited men and began incorporating them into their forces.

Italy Spring 212

The senate and the consuls decided to increase the size of the Roman army to 23 legions; to do this two new legions would need to be raised and the recruitment age was dropped, again, to below 17 and raised above 46 years. Both consuls were assigned two legions each and were tasked with gaining Capua. The praetor Sulla was given the twin task of city praetor and courts, G Flaccus was assigned to Apulia, G Nero to take command of Varro's army in Picenum and M Silanus with the previous year's 2 newly raised legions to Etruria. All new commanders were ordered to bring their armies up to full strength. For the first time the Scipio brothers were formally assigned the two new provinces in Spain and continued to control the army and navy there. Marcellus continued with the siege, Lentulus continued in Sicily, Gracchus in Lucania and Otacilius remained in command of the navy based in Sicily.

A new pontifex maximus (Chief Priest) was elected; Publius Licinius Crassus who, like Scipio Junior, was considered far too young for the post and had not even been an Aedile beforehand.

According to Livy (1965) Rome was holding hostages from the cities of Tarentum and Thurii (close to San Lorenzo Bellizzi) to ensure the cities remained loyal[22]. The hostages, with assistance, made an attempt to escape from Rome; However, they were caught and executed. This then set the scene for

---

[22] Livy is uncertain as to the year Tarentum revolts, if it did in 213, it would explain why Rome executed the hostages in 212

what happened in both cities during 212. Tarentum, following the events in Rome, decided that it was better off with Hannibal and arranged to allow Hannibal access to the city. Hannibal, on entering the city, found the Roman garrison had fled to the citadel (situated on a peninsula with the landward side protected by a wall and ditch), so he besieged the citadel by building his own wall and ditch. But the garrison was accessible from the sea, so Hannibal left a small force to ensure the garrison could not gain access to the rest of the city.

While Hannibal was dealing with Tarentum, the consuls reached Capua and began laying out their siege works; they summoned Fulvius to assist with the siege and so three Roman armies were now based around Capua. They built a number of camps and a double wall which enclosed their camps; this is similar to Julius Caesar's siege of Alesia 52 BC (Duncan B Campbell, 2005). Hannibal sent Hanno to assist Capua with food and men and he camped close to Beneventum. Fulvius was sent to Beneventum. Whilst there he learnt that Hanno had left his camp; so he attacked it and captured a large amount of the supplies that were destined for Capua. Hannibal now began to move his army north and sent cavalry to reinforce Hanno; who was now at Cominium Ocritum (Cerreto Sannita). Appius Claudius summoned Gracchus to hold Beneventum while Fulvius returned to the siege.

The praetor Cornelius, using ships, broke the Tarentum blockade and delivered both supplies and reinforcements to the garrison. While he was away from Metapontum, it changed sides. Then Thurii also changed sides as Mago, with aid from Hanno, defeated the Roman garrison which had attempted to break out of the city.

Gracchus, while at Beneventum, was lured out of the town by the promise that local Lucanain magistrates wished to meet him to discuss changing sides. He left with his bodyguard and on the way to the meeting he was ambushed by Mago's cavalry and killed along with his bodyguard. Mago went on to have more success in attacking Roman troops outside of their besieging camp, burning crops. Hannibal reached Mago and together they came to battle with part of the consul's joint army; the result was a draw. But the presence of Hannibal so close to two consuls and their army meant Rome launched a deception plan to keep Hannibal away from Capua and the consular armies.

Fulvius moved his forces to Cumae in an attempt to lure Hannibal, but he failed to move so instead Claudius moved his army and Hannibal followed. Rome also sent a scratch force to keep Hannibal occupied. It seems that Claudius led Hannibal towards this force somewhere in Lucania. Claudius returned to Beneventum and Hannibal came to blows with this force. This time Rome was the smarter of the two forces and Hannibal may well have thought he was going up against Claudius instead of the scratch force, which he defeated. Hannibal may well have believed he had destroyed one of the consular armies, as he did not return to Capua and instead headed into Apulia and attacked Fulvius Flaccus; close to Herdonea (Ordona). Fulvius was caught in his camp by Hannibal, on coming out he formed his units up into a long thin line; in an effort probably to stop his flanks being turned by Hannibal's formation, as had happened so often to Roman formations. Instead Hannibal's front line burst through the thin Roman line, and with the aid Mago and his cavalry, wiped out Fulvius' legions and allied forces. Hannibal moved back to Tarentum and failed in an attempt to take the citadel, then tried his luck at Brundisium and failed there too.

To replace the lost forces, the consuls ordered Claudius Nero and his force to march from Casilinum to Capua.

Sicily 212

Marcellus continued with his siege of Syracuse, while Himilco and Hippocrates were based inland from his forces. During the summer the naval blockade seized a ship carrying a Spartan diplomat named Damippus; who was travelling between Syracuse and Philip V of Macedon. Epicycdes, desperate for the safe return of Damippus, offered a large ransom. Marcellus, with an eye to the future; according to Livy (1965), released him for payment as Rome had plans to work with the Aetolian League against Philip V.

As a bonus during the exchange, the Romans noticed that the sea wall close to the Galeagra tower was low enough to be reached by ladder. So, during the festival of Dianna (mid- August) Marcellus ordered an attempt by a small force to scale the sea wall at night and then open the gates of the city's wall to the main Roman army. The small force gained access to the city and then took control of the gates within the Hexaplyon Tower. At dawn Marcellus' forces poured into the Epipolae section of the city[23] and sacked the quarter, they then built a camp within this quarter to defend themselves from counter attacks from the other quarters of the city, and also from a counter attack led by either Himilco or Hippocrates.

Marcellus then moved on to a fortified hill, the Euryalus, which surrendered and he now controlled the main route out of the city making it harder for Himilco's forces to enter that area of the city. Epicycdes based his forces in the Achradina; which held the palace and access to the harbour. During this period another Carthaginian general named Bomiclar, with a small fleet sailing directly from Carthage, broke the Roman blockade of port, bringing supplies. He retired back to Carthage shortly afterwards to prevent the Roman fleet from trapping him inside the harbour. Marcellus now laid siege to the Achradina; Hippocrates and Himilco entered the city and supported Epicycdes in an effort to force Marcellus out of the city. They failed and the siege around the quarter was tightened.

In autumn plague broke out inside the Achradina, killing many of the defenders including both Himilco and Hippocrates. Bomiclar made a last attempt to relieve the siege by bringing a large sized fleet with transports to Sicily, they were intercepted close to the Pachynum (Cape Passero) promontory and scattered by the Roman fleet; the transports retreated back to Carthage and Bomiclar went to Tarentum. Epicycdes escaped from Syracuse just before the Achradina surrendered. He travelled to Agrigentum to organise the defence of the port. Marcellus allowed his army to sack the Achradina, after he secured the palace and Hiero's treasury for Rome.

During the sacking of this quarter Archimedes was cut down by a Roman soldier. Marcellus, on learning of this, had Archimedes properly buried. Octacilius and the fleet remained active during the siege and raided the North African coast, storming the port of Utica and taking a number of laden grain ships back to Sicily, which enabled Marcellus to feed Syracuse and his army. Marcellus then moved on Agrigentum, which was held in a joint command by Epicycdes, another Hanno and a new general sent from Carthage; Muttines. The Carthaginians moved out and lined up on their bank of the river Himera (Salso), while Marcellus placed his men on his bank. Muttines was then called away to deal with a munity by the Numidian cavalry who had retreated to Heraclea Minor. His colleagues

---

[23] Syracuse was made up of a number of quarters each with their own internal walls and towers.

crossed the river and attacked Marcellus who easily pushed them back; he followed this up by laying siege to the port of Agrigentum.

Spain 212

During the spring Hasdrubal Barca based himself at Amtorgis, with another Hasdrubal and Mago with two more armies close by. The Scipio brothers crossed the Ebro and moved their army, along with a similar number of Spanish allies, to a position close to Amtorgis and the river Baetis. They then split up their forces; Gnaeus took 1/3 of the army and moved against Hasdrubal and Mago, while Publius, with 2/3 of the army, moved against Hasdrubal Barca. At some point before the battles the Scipio's Spanish allies abandoned them and joined the Carthaginians. As both armies were separated by some distance neither knew what was happening to the other. They both then chose the same action and refused battle with the Carthaginians; instead making camp. During the night both Roman armies attempted to retreat back towards the Ebro River. Publius' forces were noticed first and Numidian cavalry, led by Masinissa (who must have crossed sometime in the spring from North Africa), caught up with them and slowed them down while Hasdrubal's and Mago's forces caught up. They were caught in a trap as an old enemy from 217 BC's campaign season made an appearance; Indibilis and his tribe arrived on the scene blocking his exit.

Publius Scipio and his army were then destroyed. Hasdrubal Barca also caught up with Gnaeus' and his forces, pushing them to attempt to defend a hilltop position with a gentle slope. Hasdrubal was in no rush, and left his cavalry to harass the Romans while he waited for his colleagues to join him. When they did, they proceeded to massacre the Roman forces on the hill top. A few Roman survivors made it back across the Ebro River bringing with them the news of the loss of the Scipio brothers and their army, as well as the advance of a large combined Carthaginian army following up on their victories. The remaining Roman forces in Spain were collected together by a tribune named Lucius Marcius. They built a fortified camp and defended it from the Carthaginian armies; forcing them to retreat back over the Ebro River and in the process saving the two new Roman-Spanish provinces. According to Livy (1965), the people of Rome were so impressed and grateful to the tribune Marcius' actions following the huge defeat that a shield, the Marcian, was dedicated to him. It hung in the Capitoline temple in Rome until it was lost in a fire.

Winter of 212

The consul Claudius returned to Rome from Capua, leaving his colleague in charge of the on-going siege. He held the elections for the consularship and praetorship. Gnaeus Fulvius Centumalus and Publius Sulpicius Galba were elected consuls. Lucius Cornelius Lentulus, Marcus Cornelius Cethegus, Gaius Sulpicius and Gaius Calpurnius Piso were elected praetors. News had not reached Rome yet of the disaster in Spain, so Rome would have been quite pleased with itself. Syracuse was back in its control and the cost of the campaign was easily covered by part of the treasury of Hiero's that Marcellus had recovered. Capua was still under siege and it would only be a matter of time before it fell; this went a little way to cover the crushing defeats that Hannibal had inflicted on two Roman armies, probably killing close to what had been lost at Cannae. But this time Rome had a large enough army in the field to absorb the losses.

Hannibal, for the first time in 4 years, had defeated two Roman armies. It must have appeared as though Tarentum would fall at any time. Yet he had not managed to lift the siege of Capua. He may well have understood, as Rome did, that his prestige was wrapped up in the fate of the city. As long as it held out, his new allies in southern Italy felt safe; if it fell then they would question their logic in swapping sides and joining him.

So 211 could well be the decisive year in his Italian campaign as well as in Rome's campaign to regain control of southern Italy.

Chapter Five: The Second Punic War Part Three

Italy Spring 211

On the 15th March 211, the new consuls took up their new posts and with the senate they debated the next move in the war with Hannibal. The main decision was to continue with the siege of Capua and complete the conquest of Sicily.

Commander	Number of legions	Location	Previous commander
Pro-consul (P-C) Q Fulvius	2	Capua	Q Fulvius
P-C Claudius	2	Capua	Claudius
Pro-praetor (P-P) Junius	2	Etruria	Junius
P-P Sempronius	2	Cisalpine Gaul	Sempronius
P-C Marcellus	2 (take any men from the rest of Sicily as required)	Sicily	Marcellus
Praetor G Sulpicius	2 (and survivors of G Fulvius Flaccus army)	Sicily	Pro-praetor Cornelius
Praetor M Cornelius	2	Sardinia	Mucius
Octacilius	2 and fleet (100 ships)	Sicily	Octacilius
Valerius	1 and fleet (50 ships)	Greece	Valerius
Consul G Fulvius	2 new		
Consul Galba	2 new		
P-P Nero	2	Spain	Nero
Publius Cornelius Scipio	2 new	Spain	

One of the tribunes of the Plebs, S. Blaesus, laid charges of treason against the ex-praetor Gnaeus Fulvius Flaccus for allowing his command to be wiped out by Hannibal and not dying with his command. Those of Flaccus' army who had survived were punished by the senate for cowardice (they failed to die on the battlefield). In the same manner of those who had survived Cannae, the remnant was sent to Sicily for the duration of the war, before they would be allowed to step back on Italian soil. Flaccus was now to be made an example of; the people and the senate needed an example made of commanders who failed and Flaccus would be the first, and for Rome, hopefully the last.

Flaccus, knowing the penalty was death and that no one would intervene, chose exile in Tarquinii (Tarquinia) – which suited everyone, thus the matter was laid to rest. Secondly, the charges laid by the tribune, on behalf of the plebs (people), could also be interpreted as a reminder to the elite that with position comes accountability, and even in war they were still answerable to the people of Rome. Lastly, it also gave a message that a Roman commander was expected to be honourable and die, rather than report the loss of his command.

In the meantime the siege of Capua had continued through the winter and was moving into the spring. During the siege the Romans had found it hard to counter the Campanian cavalry, so they devised a joint force of spearman and cavalry. Each of the cavalry carried into battle a spearman, whom they dropped off, the spearmen then formed a line in front of the cavalry. They then launched their missiles against the enemy cavalry, breaking up their formation, at which point the Roman cavalry attacked and scattered the cavalry.

Hannibal had to then make a choice to either save Capua or take the citadel of Tarentum. He chose Capua and, leaving his baggage train behind in Bruttium, he began the march north to Capua, reached his old camp at Tifata and on route took the fort at Calatia. His plan was to launch a combined assault on the siege works around Capua. He intended an attack from the outside, whilst Boster and Hanno would strike the inner siege wall from the city.

Claudius and Q. Fulvius decided to split up their forces; Claudius with his infantry would deal with Boster and Hanno. Q Fulvius would face Hannibal and the cavalry was split between pro-praetor Nero and the tribune Flaccus; placing the cavalry in two positions clear of the walls and ditches where they could support Q Fulvius. The combined assault began, Claudius was able to push back the attackers into the city, during which he was wounded and later died from the injury. Hannibal assaulted Q Fulvius and at one point his Spanish infantry almost broke through the wall into the Roman camp. The cavalry attacked the flanks of Hannibal's army and Q Fulvius was eventually able to force Hannibal to leave the field and retire to his camp.

Q Fulvius returned to the siege with Claudius, Hannibal was unable to force his way into the city and decided on another plan. This was to draw the Roman armies away from the siege, and so he decided to attack Rome. This was probably one of his most audacious moves in the Italian campaign, catching the Romans completely off guard. He set off with his army along the Via Latina, pillaging along the route until he camped about 8 miles from Rome. Q Fulvius, on learning of Hannibal's march, set off with two legions and cavalry taking the Via Appia and, by forced marches, managed to reach Rome at about the same time as Hannibal made his camp. The senate gave the pro-consul a dispensation so that he could enter Rome at the head of an army. He brought his army in through the Porta Capena (Capua gate?) and out through the Porta Esquilina (gate that gave access to the Esquiline Hill), thereby placing his army on the east side of the city.

Hannibal, in the meantime, moved up the via Latina, then north eastward going past Rome towards Tivoli, if he was to have his camp, as Livy (1965) states, on the river Anio (Aniene); in this case Livy has probably got it wrong and Hannibal was to the east of the city opposite the location of Q Fulvius' camp. Hannibal then, with an escort of cavalry, approached the Porta Collinea (north corner of Rome) before being chased off by Roman cavalry. This would be the closet Hannibal ever came to the city of Rome. Livy (1965) then reports that both armies lined up close to the graveyards and faced each other for two days, as continually heavy rain was taken as a bad portent by the Romans; so they would not fight. In the end it was Hannibal who retreated and pulled back all the way south past Capua, before turning and heading to Rhegium (Reggio Calabria) in an attempt to storm it.

Capua quickly learned of Hannibal's retreat south and the city lost the will to fight. The senators held a meeting one evening in the summer and decided to surrender the city the next day. Most went home and killed their families and then themselves; they knew what would happen in the morning. The city surrendered the next day, the Roman army marched in, collected up all the Carthaginians as prisoners, and sent them off to be sold as slaves. The remaining senators were collected up and sent either to Cales or Teanum. The following morning, Fulvius had them all executed as an example to all Italian towns and cities that had sided with Hannibal, as to what they could expect if they did not ally themselves with Rome. The remaining inhabitants were expelled from the city, losing Roman or allied citizenship (some probably sold as slaves), and Capua became a Roman colony answerable directly to the senate; so no council was allowed to form. The city was then opened to Roman citizens and their allies to populate. Next the towns of Atella and Calatia also surrendered, the city leaders were executed for treason and the population was sold off as slaves.

Following the conquest of Capua the Italian campaign for both Rome and Hannibal went into a quiet period as both sides consolidated gains and losses. Hannibal's situation had now worsened as he had lost Capua and his allies realised that he was no longer setting the pace of the campaign in Italy. The best the allies could hope for was a stalemate and the intervention of Philip V of Macedon. Hannibal had still been unable to utilise his Gallic allies; as Rome had now stationed two legions in the north to ensure no link up.

Sicily 211

Marcellus arrived in Rome and was given an ovation (allowed to enter city with his army on horseback or on foot) as recognition of his conquest of Syracuse. During the autumn Carthage reinforced its position on the island; a number of cities sidled towards Carthage, such as Murgantia and Ergetium. During the autumn Octacilius, the commander of the fleet, died. The praetor Cornelius quickly regained control of these wayward cities and towns, then retired for the winter.

Spain 211

The news of the defeats and death of the Scipio brothers reached Rome in the spring. The senate immediately assigned the pro-praetor Nero and his legions to Spain, in order to take control while the senate and people decided on who should be the new commander of the provinces and army. Nero landed at Tarraco and took control of the army there from Marcius. In the late summer, during a campaign to regain control of the loyalty of the Celtic Iberian tribes, he found Hasdrubal Barca and his forces camped in a canyon. He blocked the entrance and Hasdrubal Barca asked for talks to discuss his surrender. Nero reckoned that he had him trapped, so decided to allow this. This proved to be a costly mistake; as Hasdrubal Barca was able to move his army out, over the rear of the canyon, avoiding the Roman forces during the night. Nero later discovered this too late to catch up with Hasdrubal Barca. As can be imagined, Nero failed to have any of the Celtic Iberian tribes return to an alliance with Rome. He returned his forces to Tarraco for the winter.

During the summer the senate and the people held an election for a new commander in Campus Martius (field of Mars). At some point the 24 year old Publius Cornelius Scipio stood up and announced his candidature for the position[24]. It is most likely that he and his family had planned this, seeding the electorate with cash to ensure their votes and that they would persuade friends and family to do the same. So Publius Cornelius Scipio was elected. Livy (1965) adds that he explained this by saying he had received portents from the gods that he should undertake this course of action. Livy then goes on to introduce a reference to Alexander the Great (Livy, 1965) who, also as a young man, went on to conquer the East, so had set precedence for young Scipio to follow as the New Roman Alexander. He was dispatched in the early autumn, with two legions, cavalry and an equal amount of allied troops and landed at Emporiae (Empúries), before he proceeded to march down to Tarraco with the fleet shadowing him, to winter with Nero and his forces. Rome was now fielding a total of 25 legions.

Greece 211/210

In either the summer or the autumn Laevinus held a conference with the Eleans (western Peloponnese), the Spartans, Attalus King of Asia, Pleuratus king of Thrace and Scerdilaedus king of Illyria and an alliance was agreed. Rome had now almost surrounded Macedon with allies. The alliance would make war with Rome's enemies (Philip V) and in return; Rome would fight with them and hand over Acarnania and all land south of Corcyra to them, whilst Rome would keep all the loot and lands north of Corcyra. Rome now began to develop a foothold in Greece. Laevinus made his first move and took control of Zacynthus (Zante), Oeniadae (Oiniades) and Nassus (Acarnania), which were handed over to his allies. Philip responded by raiding into Oricum and Apollonia, then into Pelagonia; taking the town of Sintia. He then raided Thessaly; attacking the city of Lamphorynna. Scopas, leader of the Aetolian league, moved against Acarnania as Philip was busy elsewhere; Philip quickly moved to support the city and Scopas retired.

In early spring campaigning began again, with the consul-elect Laevinus summoning all his allies to meet him outside Anticyra (Antikyra) in Locris; which was easily stormed. With Macedon

---

[24] He may well have been the only candidate

contained for the time being, Laevinus returned to Rome to be made consul. The ex-consul Sulpicius replaced Laevinus as commander of the fleet.

Winter of 211/210

The consular elections were held again. Marcus Valerius Laevinus and Marcus Marcellus were elected consuls. Publius Manlius Volso, Lucius Manlius Acidinus, Gaius Laetorius and Lucius Cincius Alimentus were elected praetors.

Italy 210

Following the ides of March the new consuls and senate met and decided that the time was right to release all long serving soldiers; both from the legions and the allies. Laevinus decided that the situation in Greece was safe enough to withdraw the one legion, but kept the fleet there to blockade Philip from any intervention in Greece or Italy. With the situation more stable in Italy, the practice of training 2 fresh legions for one year in Rome was continued, and the previous 2 legions were now considered suitable for combat and were therefore assigned to the provinces.

Marcellus took control of Italy; under him Quintus Fulvius remained in Capua, Gnaeus Fulvius in Apulia. Marcellus would also raise new legions. Laevinus took command of Sicily with the praetor Lucius Cincius taking over command of the two punishment legions in Sicily. Rome reduced its manpower from 25 legions to 21 legions. The town of Salapia also returned to side with Rome.

Marcellus began campaigning in Italy by sending a resupply fleet to the citadel of Tarentum under the command of Decimus Qvinctius. The fleet clashed with Tarentum's at Sapriportis; it was defeated and Decimus was killed. During this period the garrison of the citadel sallied out into the town when it noticed that the defenders were preoccupied; the town was sacked and the garrison, with fresh stores, returned to the citadel.

Marcellus, during the summer, captured Marmoreae and Meles; each time Hannibal lost a garrison. Over a period of time this would have become a drain on his manpower. The pro-consul Gnaeus Fulvius was close to Herdonea and either preparing to storm the town, or had just taken it when Hannibal appeared on the scene; catching the Roman army unaware. Hannibal deployed his army in the usual formation with the cavalry on either wing. Fulvius appeared not to have protected his flanks, as Hannibal used the same tactics as before and rolled up the Roman rear with his cavalry. Fulvius with his army was destroyed and Hannibal sacked Herdonea. Hannibal had, again, used the same tactics and a Roman commander had failed to learn from all the previous engagements; the danger of not protecting his flanks from the Carthaginian cavalry. The survivors who reached Marcellus, were later condemned to the punishment legions in Sicily for the duration of the war.

Marcellus, obviously incensed at the loss of two legions and allies, moved quickly to bring Hannibal to battle and regain Roman pride and the initiative from Hannibal. He caught up with

Hannibal at Numistro; both sides deployed wide lines to ensure neither side could outflank the other. The first day of battle resulted in neither army breaking the others' front lines. The next day Hannibal refused battle; leaving the Romans free to bury their dead and collect whatever spoils were left on the field. During the night Hannibal pulled out and marched towards Apulia. Marcellus waited for dawn before following; both sides continued to skirmish during the day and at night Marcellus halted whilst Hannibal tried to escape.

In the late autumn Marcellus was still chasing Hannibal, when the senate recalled him for the forthcoming elections, expecting that he had already moved his army to winter quarters. Marcellus informed them that he was unable to return as he was still chasing Hannibal and intended to continue. So the senate summoned Laevinus from Sicily instead. In the meantime King Syphax made contact directly with Rome, to inform them that he wished to renew his treaty of friendship directly with the senate. Envoys were dispatched to confirm the alliance, and also to try and gather any more dissident Numidians tribes to the Roman cause. Lastly the envoys visited Egypt to ensure that Ptolemy and Cleopatra remained neutral in the war; which they achieved.

Sicily 210

Laevinus, on arriving on the island, moved his forces to besiege Agrigentum. During the siege the Carthaginian commanders fell out with each other; Muttines and his Numidians decided to swap sides and, as part of the deal, they agreed to open the city gates to Laevinus. The revolt took place and Laevinus and his troops entered the city with little resistance, Hanno and Epicycdes escaped by ship to Carthage. The city's leaders were executed and the population sold off into slavery. Laevinus finished his campaign season by forcing any remaining allies of Carthage to surrender, or face the same fate as Agrigentum.

Sicily was now fully under Roman control and, shortly afterwards, became a Roman province. With Sicily back in Rome's control food and taxation would once again flow from the island into Rome. Laevinus dispatched the fleet under Messalla to raid Utica in North Africa. The raid was successful and a number of important prisoners were brought back to Sicily. From the prisoners Laevinus learnt that Carthage was building a new fleet with the intention of attacking Sicily. More importantly Carthage was recruiting a large force to be sent to Spain for Hasdrubal Barca to march to Italy; with which to support Hannibal. Before winter Laevinus was ordered to return to Rome after conscripting 4,000 prisoners from Sicilian jails to serve at Rhegium, in another punishment legion.

Laevinus reported this to the senate, but decided because the threat was so great he needed to return to Sicily. So, without the agreement of the senate he chose a dictator. The senate rejected the choice and demanded Marcellus elect a dictator; he chose Q Fulvius with Publius Crassus as his master of horse. The people elected Q Fulvius and Q Fabius as consuls, causing a little excitement as a dictator was elected consul, so setting a new precedence. With excellent timing the Carthaginian fleet, led by Hamiclar, raided Sardinia before winter stopped any sailing. Proving to the senate and consuls that the information they had gained from the prisoners was correct. Laelius, with his prisoners, reached Rome bringing the news of conquest of New Carthage.

Spain 210

Scipio assembled his army in the spring and, on learning that the Carthaginians were campaigning away from the coast, decided to launch an audacious assault on the capital of Bacrid Spain, New Carthage. Moving quickly along the coast, supported by the fleet under Laelius, they reached New Carthage. New Carthage lay on a peninsula jutting out into the mouth of a river (Estero long ago silted up) connected to the land by a narrow strip; on the east and south the sea, and to the west the lagoon of the Estero. Scipio built the standard siege works on the peninsula, blocking egress from the city and protecting his rear from counter attack. The fleet sailed into the lagoon and blocked the harbour. At some point Scipio learnt that the lagoon was tidal, and when the tide was out the walls of the western side were reachable and also shorter. So he launched a general assault which drew the defenders to the land wall.

Next he assigned a small force with breaching ladders to cross the lagoon and storm into the city, while he launched a diversionary attack on the land walls again. By the end of the day he had captured the city, his men plundered and he collected the stores of the Carthaginian's army; including their treasury. Secondly, he now had control of hostages for all the allied tribes of the Carthaginians. Here Livy (1965) began to again develop the character of Scipio further with his dealing of the hostage women and daughters. He acted like a man of honour, and here Livy is setting an example for his readers to emulate; he doesn't take advantage of the situation, and he even protests to one female hostage that he regards them as inviolate; like wives and daughters of a good Roman family. Here Livy is using Scipio to portray the image of what he thinks the Emperor Augustus[25] would like all patrician youths too aspire to; that of highly moral and religious men of honour.

Scipio had all the important prisoners, and Mago, sent to Rome with Laelius to announce the good news from Spain. Scipio here realised the important role played by the people of Rome in keeping him in command in Spain. So he needed to bring them good news and the spectacle of senior Carthaginian prisoners. Julius Caesar learnt this lesson; as he also understood the need for good publicity to maintain the support of the people of Rome, no matter what the patrician class thought of him.

Scipio had the defences of New Carthage strengthened, left a garrison behind and retired for the winter to Tarraco.

Italy 209

---

[25] Augustus introduced strict marriage laws for the patrician class, which meant they could only marry within that class. He also condemned his own daughter for adultery, while he continued with his many affairs

The senate and consuls agreed that the situation had stabilised enough for both consuls to operate in Italy against Hannibal. Sicily was secure in Roman hands and Philip V of Macedon was no longer a threat. So Rome could once again concentrate on Hannibal. Q Fabius was assigned to Tarentum with 2 legions; Q Fulvius Flaccus was given command of Lucania and Bruttium with 2 legions. Marcellus' command was extended for another year. Pro-consul Sulpicius remained in Greece with a fleet. Laevinus, commanding the fleet, was ordered to conduct raids against North Africa. Two new legions were recruited and based at Rome. Gaius Flaccus was sent to command in Etruria. This year 12 of the Latin colonies refused to supply men and money as they said the war had drained them completely, whereas the other 18 colonies were able to fulfil the levy. However the senate, which were unable to use force against the colonies, decided instead to ignore those that had not given them what was required.

Fabius began operations in southern Italy and used the punishment legion at Rhegium to stir up Hannibal's allies by looting and burning farms etc… finally, they were sent to try and take Caulonia. This had the desired effect and forced Hannibal to move to Caulonia. Marcellus continued with the pursuit and harrying of Hannibal's movements, in the process relieving Canusium. This time he changed his tactics and instead of allowing Hannibal to make camp at dusk, he attacked. This caught Hannibal out and both armies fought until dark, only to then retire to their camps. The next day both armies formed up, and battle commenced with both front lines holding steady; this time Hannibal used elephants to break the Roman front line. This worked for a time, until the Roman infantry regrouped and counter attacked; they encouraged the elephants to stampede back through Hannibal's lines, breaking up his front line. The Roman infantry quickly followed through and Hannibal was forced to retire from the battlefield to his camp with Roman cavalry chasing them. In the encounters so far, Marcellus and Hannibal's forces were equal in strength and so far none of the battles had proved decisive enough for one side to collapse. For Hannibal this only needed to happen once and he was finished; for Rome they could afford to lose a consular or pro-consular army or two.

Hannibal retired back toward Bruttium. The Hirpini (one of the Samnite people), Lucanians and the town of Volceii surrendered to Fulvius; who, at this time, adopted a more lenient policy and did not execute the leaders. Fabius took Manduria by storm then marched to Tarentum and in conjunction with the Sicilian fleet under Laevinus; they stormed the port, aided by treachery from within the city allowing him access through one of the gates. The port was sacked and most of the garrison was slaughtered. The punishment legion from Rhegium had served its purpose and kept Hannibal away from Tarentum and it was destroyed by him at Caulonia. Hannibal retired back to Metapontum.

Spain 209

In the spring Hasdrubal Barca moved his army to Baecula[26], Scipio had already been on the move with his army and caught Hasdrubal in camp. This may well have been part of the reinforcement army sent from Carthage, as the location of the battle may well point to Hasdrubal Barca already moving this army north; attempting to avoid the Roman army in Tarraco. The result was that Hasdrubal retreated in the dusk from his camp, up a steep hilltop and deployed his army in defensive positions on the hill. The next morning Scipio, with the army, stormed up the steep slope; defeating Hasdrubal's light infantry who were holding a lower position on the hill. The assault continued with Scipio and Laelius splitting up the army and outflanking the hilltop positions, assaulting them and driving Hasdrubal from the slope; this left most of his army dead or captured behind him.

Scipio, well aware of the need to build up his Spanish allies, released all Spanish troops that had been captured. In return Livy (1965) suggests that they proclaimed Scipio as their Roman king. Scipio then rebuked them for their action and informed them that Rome had no kings, that his power came from the senate; who had given him the power to command; *imperator*. This story has more to do with the political situation following Augustus' defeat of Mark Anthony. At this point Augustus was now the sole ruler of the Roman Empire; instead of becoming king he laid down his power to the senate, but they quickly refused to accept it and so Augustus retained the power of *imperator* "for life–Emperor". This familiar event, rolled into the context of his character building, meant that Livy could connect with his audience. The accuracy of this event is easily questionable.

Among the African prisoners who were to be sold into slavery, they found the grandson of the Gela, the Numidian ally of Carthage, and the nephew of Masinissa. Scipio at first decided to keep him as a hostage, but saw a chance to lever at least Masinissa away from Carthage. So he released him and sent him back to Masinissa loaded with gifts.

Scipio, following the battle, retired back to Tarraco; there he met the likes of Indibilis (one of those allies of Carthage who was involved in the killing of his father and uncle) and Mandonius. Both along with their tribes came over to Rome's side. One plausible reason for the change of sides was that Scipio had been holding their wives and children since he had captured New Carthage. Scipio spent the rest of the year developing alliances with other Celtiberian tribes, as well as deploying a small force to watch the Pyrenees's passes. Scipio was obviously well aware that Hasdrubal would, at some point; attempt to leave Spain en-route to Hannibal.

Hasdrubal Barca, following the defeat, retired back to Gades with his allies to rebuild the army and prepared to cross into Gaul. Masinissa was left further east to harass any Spanish tribes changing sides.

---

[26] The location of this battle is still a topic of debate among classical historians; see http://digital.csic.es/bitstream/10261/32799/1/Baecula.%20An%20archaeological%20analysis%20of%20the%20location%20of%20a%20battle%20of%20the%20second%20punic%20war.pdf, for a good argument for placing it in the valley of the river Baetis almost due north of New Carthage.

Italy 208

The war was about to enter the tenth year, so far Hannibal had been able to roam at will in southern Italy; between 25 and 21 legions, numerous consuls and pro-consuls had, so far, failed to defeat him. Rome was gradually regaining lost towns and cities in the south, but not fast enough to cause Hannibal any problems with supplies or contact with Carthage. Sicily was now a Roman province and Spain was slowly developing into new provinces. This, for Rome, was one real positive aspect of the long war with Hannibal and Carthage. Therefore, it was no surprise that one of the Tribune of the Plebs, representing the will of the people of Rome, laid charges against Marcellus and, by implication, the whole patrician class, that he (they) were failing to prosecute the war with due earnest. Instead they were enjoying the unprecedented amount of power and wealth the continued war brought them. The charges were thrown out, but the point had been made that the patrician class was developing into a complete oligarchy and felt no qualms in disregarding the 'will' of people; the senate was gradually becoming the centre of power not the assemblies.

The consular elections were held and Marcellus was elected consul again (fifth) with Titus Quinctius Crispinus. The praetors were P Publius Licinius, Publius Licinius Varus, Sextus Julius Caesar and Quintus Claudius.

The number of legions remained constant at 21.

Commander	Number of legions	Location
Marcellus	2	Venusia (Venosa)
Crispinus	2	Lucania
Caesar	2 (Punishment)	Sicily
Claudius	2	Tarentum
Flaccus	1	Capua
Philo	2	Gaul
P-P Tubulus	2	Etruria
P-P G Aurunculeius	2 plus most of Scipio's fleet	Sardinia
Scipio and Silanus	Army of Spain	Spain
Laevinus	Fleet	Sicily
Sulpicius	Fleet	Greece
Varus	2 new legions	Rome

In the spring word reached Rome that a disturbance had broken out in the town of Arretium (Arezzo) in Etruria. Tubulus was ordered to enter the town and seize hostages to ensure good behaviour; he did this, placing one of his legions in the town. The senate, concerned, sent Varro to investigate; he visited the town and brought back 120 town senators with their families to ensure no more problems within the town. Following his report, he was sent back to garrison the town with one of the city legions, freeing Tubulus to defend Etruria.

Crispinus reached Lucania and Marcellus reached Venusia when word reached Marcellus that Hannibal was approaching the town. Crispinus moved his forces to Venusia and both consular armies made camp, about the same time that Hannibal arrived on the scene and made camp as well. With Hannibal now facing two consular armies, it was decided to make a move on Locri using the troops based in Tarentum and part of the Sicilian fleet, under the command of Lucius Cincius. The troops were ambushed on route to Locri and retired back, leaving Cincius with the fleet to mount a siege; which he did.

Hannibal had again placed his camp with a hill between his position and that of the Romans. He then placed some of his Numidian cavalry in the woods on the hill, to watch the Romans and disperse any attempt to take the hill. Marcellus had also realised the importance of the hill; with his fellow consul and most of his command staff and bodyguards, he decided to reconnoitre the hill. Marcellus had under-estimated Hannibal yet again, and as many of his earlier consular colleagues, had discovered Roman overconfidence was one of Hannibal's greatest offensive weapons.

Marcellus and his company rode straight into an ambush.

Marcellus' son and a wounded Crispinus were the only commanders to make it back to the Roman camp. The Roman army suffered a major loss of confidence and its command structure completely broke down. Marcellus' son took command of his father's army and the wounded Crispinus, who had to be carried in a litter, ordered a retreat to a range of higher hills where they dug in.

Hannibal decided not to follow up on his success and instead pulled out and made his way towards Locri, sending his Numidian cavalry on to back up the defenders of the city. On route he attempted to force Salapia to surrender to him, they refused and he moved on. Mago, defending the city, was now able to launch a counter attack with the aid of the cavalry and drove Cincius and his troops back to their ships. Cincius returned to Sicily.

Crispinus, on learning of the failure, decided that a general retreat was in order and headed back to Capua. He sent a message to the senate informing them of the twin disasters, and that he was too ill to make the journey back to Rome even for the consular elections. The young Marcellus was ordered to hold a position close to Venusia.

Claudius moved his forces to protect Tarentum. Marcus Valerius, commanding another part of the fleet, raided North Africa, sacking Clupea and defeating a Carthaginian fleet sent to intercept him.

The senate sent a delegation to Crispinus made up of Pollio, Cincius and Caesar to ask him to elect a dictator to oversee the election, and to replace him should he die of his wounds.

Greece 208

During the summer Philip intervened on the side of the Achaeans against the Spartans and Aetolians. He joined the Achaeans; together they defeated the Aetolians under Pyrrhias at Lamia and forced them to attend a peace conference he organised at Phalara, on the Malian Gulf. Here Philip brought together envoys from his main allies and the Aetolian league, where he attempted to settle the outstanding issues. Since the Aetolians had lost the last battle, they asked for 30 days grace to decide their response. They met again at Aegium (Aigio), where Philip now demanded that they should hand back all sized territory. The Aetolians, now with news that Attalus king of Asia

(South western Turkey) and Rome were coming to their aid, demanded that Philip and his allies return all captured land. Both sides refused giving Philip what he wanted; an excuse to become fully involved in Greek affairs, while acting as a champion of the Achaeans.

The Greek states may well have been planning to have the major powers become involved as a way of balancing the power of Macedon, but not to the extent of being occupied by any of the three powers. Macedon, since Alexander the Great, had been the main power, but the continued civil war between the Macedonian generals following Alexander's death had weakened Macedon. The results of the Greek states' actions were to bring the major powers into the region. Greece was now going to be the site of a regional power struggle. The winner would gain control of Greece and the surrounding region.

Philip also had plans for the war, he had made an alliance with King Prusias of Bithynia (a major enemy of Attalus) and had a received a force of Carthaginian warships to add to his own fleet. Sulpicius now made his move and raided the coast around Corinth. This caused Philip, who was attending the Nemean Games in Argos, to leave and bring his forces to Corinth. Sulpicius pulled out and moved his forces to Elis. Philip was then forced to follow him overland to Elis, where he was joined by his allies. Both alliances clashed with Philip and his company were defeated; Philip withdrew to a fortress at Pyrgus. During this period revolts flared up on the borders of Macedonia and Illyria; forcing Philip to return home, and taking him out Greece for the rest of the year. Sulpicius and Attalus wintered at Aegina.

Italy winter 208

During the late autumn or early winter the consul Crispinus died of his wounds; he had already named Titus Manlius Torquatus as Dictator and Gaius Servilius as his master of horse. The dictator held the elections for the consulships and praetorships in Rome. Gaius Claudius Nero and Marcus Livius were elected consuls and Lucius Porcius Licinius, Gaius Mamilius and the brothers Gaius and Aulus Hostilius Cato were elected praetors.

Rome had been battered by Hannibal yet again, two consuls killed, but luckily not their armies. Still, Rome had not been able to produce commanders with the ability to defeat Hannibal outright and, with the war entering its 11th year, this was a major problem. Hannibal had survived yet another year and had inflicted a major dent in Roman morale.

Italy 207

The senate sent L. Manlius to Greece in order to report on the situation there, he was also ordered to visit refugees from South Italy and Sicily and encourage them to return (Rome needed to boost the economy of the regions it had re-conquered), he was also representing Rome at the Olympic Games to be held in the summer. News also reached Rome that Hasdrubal Barca had departed Spain with a large force and was marching into Gaul, then into Italy some time later in the year. The senate decided that Livius should deal with Hasdrubal Barca, while Nero dealt with Hannibal. The census was also completed and showed that the Roman male population had decreased since the last census; with a total of just over 137,000. The news meant that Nero needed to again recruit slaves, as there were not enough Roman males available to fill the new levy.

Commander	Number of legions	Region or city
Nero	2	Rome then Southern Italy
Livius	2	northern Italy
A Cato	2	Sardinia
Scipio	4	Spain
Tubulus	1	Capua
Varro	2	Etruria
Fulvius	2	Bruttium
Q Claudius	2	Tarentum
Mamilius	2 (punishment)	Sicily
Porcius	2	Cisalpine Gaul

In late spring Rome was still recruiting and training the new legions, when word reached it that Hasdrubal Barca had entered Cisalpine Gaul and was besieging Placentia. Livius had remained in Rome until he had news of what Hasdrubal was going to do. Hannibal also began to move northward, but suffered a major ambush at the hands of Tubulus and Q Claudius, who had also been moving as quickly as they could to catch up with Hannibal. Rome had been caught out by the brothers, who had moved much quicker than expected, throwing Rome into confusion, as to which brother presented the gravest threat.

Nero moved his forces to Venusia giving orders that Tubulus and Q Claudius should join him there. Once all three commanders and their armies had met up, Nero sent Tubulus back with half of the army to Capua where he had ordered Fulvius to take command. The plan seemed to have been for Nero to stop Hannibal at all costs from linking up with his brother. If he failed to stop him, then Fulvius and the rest of the army were to attempt it. In the meantime Livius would move to intercept Hasdrubal once his route was known. Hannibal, now aware of the size of the Roman forces going up against him, pulled into his army as many of the garrisons as he could spare. He headed to Grumentum where Nero was already moving to intercept him.

Both armies camped; this time Nero used the night to his advantage and placed infantry on a row of low hills close to the area where the battle was likely to take place. The next day Nero moved rapidly out of camp and did not wait for Hannibal to fully deploy his troops before attacking; this had the desired effect and Hannibal's troops, out of formation, began to fall back towards their camp. At this point the infantry in the hills came down and attacked the Carthaginian army, causing a rout back to their camp. Hannibal then refused to battle for the next couple of days, before retiring under the cover of darkness into Apulia. Nero moved after him and the cavalry skirmished, but Hannibal was able to stay in front until he reached Metapontum; where he collected more troops then doubled back heading now towards Canusium.

Nero, now aware that Hannibal had bypassed him, ordered Fulvius to defend Lucania in the event that he was unable to bring Hannibal into battle. Hannibal made camp close to Canusium. Nero reached the location and did the same.

Hasdrubal, in the meantime, gave up with Placentia and continued south. He sent messages to his brother; informing him of the route and his hope to meet in Umbria. One of these messages was intercepted however by Rome, giving them the vital intelligence they needed to counter both brothers. Livius and the senate decided to intercept Hasdrubal at Narina (Narni). Livius moved out of Rome; taking all available soldiers with him. Nero also decided to join Livius at Narina and left with about a quarter of his army. Both consuls actually met up outside Sena (Siena) then moved across the Apennines to intercept Hasdrubal in Picenum. They located him and made camp opposite his location. Hasdrubal realised that he was facing a much larger army than he expected and, instead of forming up for battle, he attempted to retire back over the River Metaurus (Metauro).

The consuls reacted by sending their cavalry to disrupt the river crossing, while moving the infantry up to the location as fast as they could. Hasdrubal reformed his lines as best he could and both armies clashed. Nero, taking troops from the Roman right wing, brought them back behind the Roman rear and swung back around to hit the Carthaginian right wing from the flank. The unexpected strike had the desired effect and the Carthaginian right wing collapsed in on the centre. Nero was then able to attack the rear of the Carthaginian army. The result was the destruction of Hasdrubal Barca and the reinforcements for Hannibal. Rome now had revenge for the death of the Scipio brothers and its first real decisive victory in Italy against the Carthaginians.

Nero, following the battle, moved his forces back to Canusium and re-joined the rest of his army. He also decided to let Hannibal know what had occurred, by having his pickled brother's head thrown at the Carthaginian camp.

In Sicily Laevinus continued his naval campaign against North Africa; attacking Utica and the area around Carthage, destroying a Carthaginian fleet and returning with a number of captured vessels.

Spain 207

With Hasdrubal Barca removed, Scipio now only had two Carthaginian armies to deal with and another Hasdrubal, unrelated to the Barca clan, was based in Spain.

During 208 Roman control extended further along the Mediterranean coastline from New Carthage; with the effect that Carthage no longer maintained a fleet in Spain. Scipio had already dispatched most of his fleet to Sardinia. Carthage sent a new general to support Mago, another Hanno; they seemed to have been based in central Spain, whilst the other Hasdrubal had been based in the south of the country. So in the spring of 207 Scipio split his forces between Silanus and himself. Silanus was tasked with defeating Mago and Hanno, whilst Scipio moved against this other Hasdrubal. Silanus caught Mago and Hanno in camp training a new army; he defeated them, capturing Hanno, while Mago fled to Gades with the survivors.

Scipio attempted to bring Hasdrubal to battle, but he avoided Scipio. Scipio then split his command with his brother Lucius who was tasked with taking Orongis. While Scipio attempted to catch up with Hasdrubal, Lucius took the town; eventually Scipio was at the end of the summer and retired back from southern Spain to Tarraco. In the autumn he sent Lucius back to Rome with Hanno, other Carthaginian prisoners and loot. Scipio again made sure that the people of Rome were aware of his victories in Spain and so continued his prolonged propaganda campaign to ensure he became the most important military commander in the war.

Greece 207

Attalus and Sulpicius combined their forces for the summer campaign and decided on attacking the island of Euboea; their first move was to the island of Lemnos in the northern Aegean. Philip V reacted to this move by bringing his forces to meet his allies at Demetrias (close to modern Volos). In the meantime the Aetolians had built defences to block the pass of Thermopylae; in an attempt to stop Philip moving his army south and crossing the causeway onto Euboea. Attalus landed close to Oreus on Euboea, while Sulpicius blocked the port. They quickly seized the port after its garrison was betrayed and surrendered in exchange for safe passage. They attempted to besiege Chalcis, but found the defences too strong, Attalus then took Opus. Philip then moved his army to support Euboea and easily broke through the defences at Thermopylae; Attalus retired as Philip crossed onto the island. Philip also sent troops who stormed Thronium in Epirus. Philip now deployed his ace; his ally Prusias of Bithynia attacked Asia, forcing Attalus to retire back to Asia to defend his kingdom. Philip now only had the Romans and Aetolians to deal with.

Sulpicius sailed back to Aegina, following Attalus' sudden withdrawal. Machanidas of Sparta used the opportunity to raid the Eleans, disrupting the preparations for the games. This forced Philip V to move from one side of Greece to the other. Once Machanidas had retired back to Sparta, Philip again met up with his allies and the Carthaginian ships; together they sailed around Greece, landed on Euboea and he retook Oreus then retired back to Demetrias for the winter to build up his fleet.

Sulpicius, lacking resources to deal with Philip V outright, achieved one vital aim; he kept him occupied in Greece and out of Italy by using hit and run tactics, forcing Philip to be the one on the defensive all summer.

Italy winter 207

Both consuls returned to Rome in time to hold the elections; Livius brought his army with him, as there was no longer any major threat in the north, while Nero left his troops at Canusium. They were both granted a triumph for the defeat of Hasdrubal. All soldiers who had fought in the battle were given a bonus and the remaining loot was placed in the treasury. The elections were held with Quintus Caecilius Metellus and Lucius Venturius Philo elected consuls, while Gaius Servilius, Marcus Caecilius Metellus, Tiberius Claudius Asellus and Quintus Mamilius Turrinus were elected Praetors.

Spring 206

The senate decided that both consuls should concentrate their efforts in Bruttium. The strategy was a return to the Fabian one of containing Hannibal, resisting battle and starving him of support by removing as many of his allies left in Southern Italy as they could.

Commander	Number of legions	Location	Previous commander

Metellus	2	Bruttium	Nero
Philo	2 (recruit men to fill gaps)	Bruttium	Livius
P-C Livius	2 (ex-slave)	Etruria	P-P G Terentius
Turrinus	2	Cisalpine Gaul	Porcius
G Servilius	2 (punishment) + 30 ships	Sicily	
Aulus Hostilius	2	Rome	From Sardinia
Asellus	1 (new)	Sardinia	
Q. Claudius	2	Tarentum	Q Claudius
G Tubulus	2	Capua	
P-C Laevinus	Fleet minus 30	Rome	Laevinus (Sicily)
Sulpicius	Fleet	Greece	Sulpicius
Scipio	4	Spain	Scipio

The senate and consuls now made it a priority to bring back the citizen farmers/ peasants to the land and bring central and Northern Italy back into production. This had to be enforced as many were refugees living in Rome where they had found work, accommodation and may well have found urban life better than the countryside. The problem of land would lead to a number of major crises in Rome between the patrician and the citizen (soldiers) class; who had, in most cases, left their land to fight, or been granted land as part of their pension. If the land was left unused then anyone could take it over as long as they paid rent. With the shortage of manpower a lot of this land would be unused, so the rich gradually took control of it and found that with the large amount of slaves for sell, thanks to the war, they could farm on a large scale without employing local labour, as well as making small farms uneconomically. So a vicious economic cycle began leading to the major crises that would beset Rome for the rest of the republican period.

Both consuls joined together at Consentia and moved through Lucania which, seeing how the tide was turning yet again in Rome's favour, re-joined the winners. They confined Hannibal into a small region of Bruttium and avoided battle. Secondly, as planned, they began to slowly starve him of resources, which coincided with Carthage making Spain a priority. Hannibal's situation was now grave, Carthage was more concerned with Spain, his alliance with Philip V had been thwarted by Sulpicius containing him in Greece, and of course the loss of his brother and his reinforcements must have had an effect on him and his army's morale.

Spain 206

Scipio, now aware that Hasdrubal Barca was dead and his army was out of Spain, had only two armies to deal with; that of the other Hasdrubal who had retired to Gades to rebuild his army and Mago Barca who was in the central region of Spain recruiting local troops. Scipio sent Silanus to collect allied troops and arranged for him to meet at Castulo; from there they would move against either Mago or Hasdrubal. By the time Scipio reached Castulo, he already knew that Mago Barca and Hasdrubal had met up close to Ilipa (close to Seville), so he headed there.

Masinissa and Mago Barca harassed Scipio's approach. Both armies camped opposite each other; over a couple of days, according to Livy (1965), they formed up but neither side would start the battle. Whatever the truth is, Scipio planned his battle very well and adopted Hannibal's usual tactic that he had used against the Romans at Cannae. At dawn on the day of the battle, Scipio sent out his Velites and cavalry to harass the Carthaginians as they deployed for battle. This had the effect of allowing him to adopt a new formation, giving the Carthaginians very little chance to adapt their deployment to his. He placed his weak allied infantry in the centre with them in a concave shape, (Hannibal's convex deployment meant they folded into a concave shape under pressure) with his heavy infantry on either wing, the cavalry and light infantry were recalled just before the battle got under way and placed on either wing to counter Carthaginian cavalry.

As Scipio's army advanced, the Carthaginian centre (made of their best infantry) had to advance faster to hit the concave shaped allied infantry. In the process they left their flanks, which were guarded by their allied troops, highly exposed to the best of the Roman infantry. The Roman cavalry was able to hold the Carthaginian cavalry; removing them from the battle. The Carthaginian allies quickly collapsed under pressure and either fled the field, or moved into the rear of the Carthaginian infantry, quickly followed by the Romans. The Carthaginians found that they were swiftly surrounded on all sides by the Roman army and were annihilated.

Rome now had a commander equal to that of Hannibal.

The remnant of the Carthaginian army fled back to their camp chased by the Roman cavalry. Scipio rested his army, allowing Hasdrubal and Mago Barca to flee back towards Gades. When he was ready he began his pursuit, catching up with Hasdrubal and Mago Barca; who had fortified themselves on top of a hill. Scipio left Silanus with part of the army to starve out the survivors, as he decided it was not worth the causalities in storming the hill. Hasdrubal and Mago Barca escaped and made their way back to Gades.

Scipio took the rest of his army back towards Tarraco. Masinissa and his Numidians, aware that they had been abandoned, now offered their services to Scipio who accepted them, as they were some of the best cavalry in the war. Shortly after Scipio had left Silanus, the survivors surrendered to him. Once in Tarraco, Scipio began to plan for the future and he made contact again with Syphax in North Africa; who had changed sides again. Scipio now saw North Africa as the next logical step for Rome to make if it was to defeat Carthage and Hannibal. So all the allies he could separate from Carthage would make that campaign much easier.

According to Livy (1965) he visited Syphax in North Africa at the same time that Hasdrubal was there on his way from Gades to Carthage. Here Livy, using the custom of hospitality, had the two recent enemies meet each other under Syphax's roof. Livy then portrayed Scipio as not only an excellent general, whose enemies even respected him, but as a great diplomat engaging with his enemy, yet not losing his temper or giving affront to his host. Syphax was obviously finding out which guest was going to give him the better deal as an ally. In the end he decided that Scipio's offer was the best. It also shows how Livy portrays, yet again, non-Romans (barbarians) as devious characters who have no honour or sense of loyalty.

Scipio, back in Spain, decided that the war was over and Bacrid Spain was no more. So he sent his brother Lucius back to Rome again with the good news, loot and prisoners. Scipio now faced a major crisis; with victory would the senate recall him back to Rome and deprive him of the army he had built up there? Back in Rome without the army, he was essentially just another very rich and well-connected politician, who had to return to the magistrate wrung to gain promotion. Yet he may well have been considering this, and as the people had been used to before, he may well have been deliberately cultivating their favour with his constant good news, loot and prisoners since he took over. Was he now to be the people's choice to continue the war in North Africa? This also must have crossed his mind in the autumn of 206, as he prepared to exact Rome's revenge on two towns that he had decided to make an example of for their betrayal of Rome.

He sent part of the army under Marcius to surround the town of Castulo, while he went first to deal with Iliturgi. He besieged Iliturgi and quickly broke in, he ordered his army to butcher everyone inside the town as an example. When he was finished he marched to Castulo, well aware that news of his punishment had reached the town already. Once he arrived the citizens of the town quickly handed over the Carthaginian garrison to Scipio and surrendered. Scipio, knowing that the fate of Iliturgi had served its purpose, accepted the surrender and did not butcher the inhabitants. Marcius was then assigned the task of bringing into alliance with Rome any remaining Spanish tribes; the task would be much easier now as they had two examples to consider of how Rome treated their enemies. He then moved onto Gades and laid siege to it.

At some point in the summer, following his return to New Carthage, he became ill; probably after his return from North Africa. With his senior commanders away, there seemed to have been a problem with paying the troops. This caused a revolt by the garrison at Sucro. Following Scipio's recovery the army was paid and the garrison was marched down to New Carthage in disgrace. The garrison was then paraded at dawn in New Carthage surrounded by the main army. The ring leaders were dragged out into the centre and brutally executed as an example to any soldier who thought of becoming a mutineer. Mandonius and his brother Indibilis either began a revolt, or began planning one for the following year. It was put down in 205, leaving Indibilis dead, Mandonius imprisoned and the tribe forced to pay a double tax for that year.

Laelius was sent with the Spanish fleet to assist in the siege of Gades, reaching Carteia (San Roque), he intercepted a Carthaginian fleet. His appearance caused them to scatter; it may well have been Mago Barca who had pulled out of Gades with whatever forces he had left and sailed into the Mediterranean, making land on the island of Ebusus (Ibiza) part of the Balearic Islands for the winter, before heading to Genoa in the spring of 205. Before the autumn, Gades surrendered following Mago's departure and Scipio, with Bacrid Spain now completely in Roman hands, was summoned to Rome to give an account of his actions in Spain since taking up his command. He left pro-praetors Acidinus and Lentulus to run the two provinces until new governors were appointed by the senate in the spring. Scipio received a hero's welcome on his return; he had secured popular support as he had hoped for. With part of his share of the spoils he paid for a number of games to be held in Rome.

Winter 206

Unsurprisingly Scipio was made a consul and his colleague was the other young, upcoming man Publius Crassus. Praetors were to be Spurius Lucreteius, Gnaeus Octavius, Gnaeus Servilius Caepio and Lucius Aemilius Papus.

For Hannibal and Carthage the campaign to destroy Rome had come to a disastrous conclusion in Spain. Hannibal was now completely confined into a small area of Bruttium, and Carthage now had reason to fear that Rome, sooner or later, would be coming to call. Rome had already been recruiting Numidian allies and the only reason for this was as part of a plan to attack the city. Hannibal and Carthage had badly miscalculated Rome's ability to recover from a series of disastrous defeats, and to be able to field five times as many legions as she had started the war with. Carthage's resources, unlike Rome's, were now in rapid decline following the loss of Spain. It must have occurred to the senate in Carthage that the war, which had begun so promisingly, now very much resembled the First Punic war. Carthage's main commander Hannibal was stuck, just as his father had been in enemy territory, though this time in Bruttium rather than Sicily. The loss of Sicily had so crippled Carthage that she had to end the war or face total collapse. Could Carthage and Hannibal pull the proverbial 'rabbit out of a hat' trick and turn the tables on Rome again?

For Rome, 206 followed on from the good year of 207 with two complete victories and, most importantly, Spain with its enormous agriculture and mineral resources. Rome now had a completely new source of revenue from which to pay for the war. This meant that time was on Rome's side, she could even afford to rest, let Hannibal and his army starve to death and watch as the same thing slowly happened to Carthage's economy. This, as in the First Punic War, would bring her to her knees begging for an end to the war on Rome's terms, which included the handing over of Hannibal and payment for the cost of the war as a minimum condition.

Chapter Six End Game

Spring and Summer 205

In the spring the new consuls and praetors met with the senate and were assigned their posts for the year. Scipio was assigned Sicily, just as he had wanted. He then announced he would use the island as a base for his attack on Carthage. As Livy (1965) reports, the senate was unhappy that Scipio had usurped their power by assigning himself North Africa. Q. Fabius here represented the view in the senate that Rome could afford to wait for Hannibal and Carthage to throw in the towel without the risk of further defeats, which would only prolong the conflict. Fabius represented the conservative strategic view for ending the war and would be, in character, a man who would later earn the title of 'the delayer'. Scipio on the other hand, knowing he had the support of the people and his fellow consul, presented the view for a fast and decisive strike against Carthage and in the process force Hannibal to leave Italy to defend his mother city.

To further his case, Scipio reminded the senate that he had two Numidian tribes already as his (meaning Rome's) allies. So he, unlike previous commanders, would be landing in territory that was not completely hostile. He also reminded the senate that continual naval raids over the last few years had shown that Carthage was now a very weak naval power and would be unable to oppose the landing, or blockade his forces in North Africa.

The senate voted to allow Scipio to extend his command to North Africa, but refused to fund the campaign, instead he was allowed to appeal to the allies of Rome for support and use his own considerable family wealth to pay for the cost of the war. The allies came to his aid, soldiers who had been discharged from Spain also reenlisted, Scipio was a popular commander and his string of victories meant he would have no trouble in recruiting men; with victory came profit.

Crassus was assigned to Bruttium with four legions to ensure that Hannibal did not go anywhere. Praetor Lucretius was sent to Cisalpine Gaul to deal with Mago Barca, should the last brother of Hannibal try and enter Italy. Aemilius was to be governor of Sicily, G. Octavius to Sardinia and Caepio in Rome to raise the two new city legions. Lastly the senate, in thanks for two great victories, sent a large amount of tribute to Apollo at the Delphi temple as thanks, also to ensure that Apollo kept up the good work.

In the spring, Mago Barca landed and took control of Genoa and began to try and unite the local Ligurian tribes to Carthage's side, but found himself involved in inter-tribal wars. The senate, not wanting to risk any chance of Mago Barca causing problems in Italy, sent the pro-consul Laevinus with the two city legions to Arretium, while Lucretius made Ariminum his base.

Scipio began assembling his forces in Sicily, having a new fleet constructed, and moved to the island. He sent Laelius with part of the fleet to Hippo Diarrhytus (Bizerte in modern Tunisia) to stir up the Carthaginians and also make contact with the Numidians. The result was that Carthage suddenly realised how grave the threat really was, made contact with his allies and ex-allies (such as Syphax) and begun to try and buy back their loyalty. The city of Locri revolted over its treatment by the Roman army and for a time welcomed a Carthaginian garrison under the command of Hamiclar. As was to be expected Rome reacted and quickly retook part of the city, leaving the Carthaginians in one part.

Hannibal moved his forces to support Hamilcar, Scipio also intervened and sent more troops to Locri. Hamilcar abandoned the city and fell back to join Hannibal. Scipio left Pleminius (with troops from Rhegium) with a garrison in the city; he then continued the abuse of the city. The city sent a delegation to the senate in Rome to complain about Pleminius' conduct and Scipio, for failing to investigate the causes of the revolt (behaviour such as Pleminius was continuing with).

In Greece Philip V made a treaty with the Aetolians, removing them from their alliance with Rome. Following the news of this, the pro-consul Sempronius was sent to Greece with 2 legions and 35 ships to renew the war and bring the Aetolians back to Rome's side. On his arrival Sulpicius was relieved of his command and sent back to Rome. Sempronius landed at Dyrrachium (Durres) and from there they advanced, with part of his army, towards Dimallum to support the local tribe; the Parthini (Illyrian tribe), against Philip V by reaching it before Philip could.

In the meantime Sempronius had dispatched Laetorius to raid and harass the Aetolians, as well as remind them to whom their first loyalty was. The result was that Philip V met with Sempronius at Phoenice (close to Finiq in modern Albania). Terms were agreed; Rome would now control the land of the Parthini along with the towns/ forts of Dimallum, Bargullum and Eugenium, while Philip would gain control of the Atintania tribe. Two leaders then informed their allies of the decision they had made; the peace of Phoenice. For Rome they gained further control of Illyria and removed Philip V from the orbit of Carthage for the time being, which also meant that Hannibal no longer had any chance of support coming from Greece. For Philip V, he regained the hegemony of Greece for the time being. They probably signed the agreement in the winter of 204, which would allow Sempronius to return with the treaty for the senate to ratify at the same time he became consul.

In the autumn, the army of Licinius was struck down by disease, stopping him returning to Rome for the winter elections. Scipio was still in Sicily and either unwilling or unable to go to Rome. So Metellus was appointed temporary dictator and his army was disbanded and sent home. The outbreak of disease in the army seemed to have been the last straw for the senior priests in Rome and together with senate they had the board of ten consult the sibylline books, as a result it was decided that Rome needed a new, more powerful, goddess to bring more divine sanction to Rome. So a delegation was sent to Attalus in Asia to ask for the Cybele (great Earth Mother) to be removed from Pessinus (Ballihisar in modern Anatolia) and transported to Rome. Attalus sent the goddess (a sacred stone) to Rome with a delegation of senior Roman senators.

The new consuls were Marcus Cethegus and Publius Sempronius Tuditanus (in Greece) with Tiberius Claudius Nero, Marcus M. Ralla, Lucius Scribonius Libo and Marcus Pomponius Matho as praetors elect.

Italy Spring 204

In the spring the new consuls took over and were assigned to Italy; Eugenium with an army was sent to Etruria to protect it from Mago Barca. Sempronius was sent down to Bruttium with orders to raise fresh troops to replace those discharged and too ill, or dead. The praetor Marcius was assigned to Rome, Libo to Cisalpine Gaul also to keep Mago Barca contained, Matho was sent to Sicily and Nero to Sardinia. Scipio was now made a pro-consul and given another year to deal with Carthage. P Licinius was also sent to Bruttium with 2 legions and Livius and Lucretius were also dispatched north with the task of briefly watching over Mago. It is assumed that Scipio must have been in Rome in the spring and this time was available, and ordered, to conduct the Great Mother Goddess from Ostia, up the Tiber to Rome; where she was set up in the temple of Victory on the Palatine Hill on the ides of April (15th).

The senate, with the agreement of the consuls, also began to repay the war loans and that year (204) paid off one third of the debt, with another third to be paid in 202 and cleared in 200. The income from Spain and Sicily was already beginning to make a real difference to the Roman economy. The delegation from Locri was then seen by the senate and their complaints were aired in public. A senatorial delegation was sent to Locri to investigate their complaints; they had Pleminius and 32 of his colleagues arrested and sent to Rhegium, then by boat to Rome; to face trial. Pleminius died in prison before the trial was finished. Scipio was exonerated by the commission.

Carthage 204

Carthage, knowing full well that Rome would invade probably sometime that year, sent Hasdrubal to complete his new alliance with Syphax and support him in his on-off civil war with Masinissa. To complete the pact and ensure that Syphax stayed loyal, Hasdrubal gave him his daughter Sophonisba (she had been betrothed to Masinissa till he broke his alliance with Carthage in Spain). So Hasdrubal was also offering Masinissa's wife-to-be, which may well have made the alliance more satisfying to Syphax, as he now had something that Masinissa was once promised. Livy (1965) also manages to slip into this section another sly comment concerning not just barbarians, but the Numidians in particular, as being driven by their passion for violence and lust. This will be his underlying theme whenever he discusses them (again in contrast not only to the Roman character but especially Scipio's character).

Syphax then sent a delegation to see Scipio. They announced to him that their alliance was over and if he, Scipio, should be so bold as to set foot in Africa, Syphax's guarantee of friendship was over and he would be his enemy. For Scipio this was bad news, as he had based most of his invasion plans on having the area to the west of Carthaginian territory in friendly hands; thereby protecting his flank from attack. Luckily for Scipio, Masinissa was still his ally and was, at present, based between Syphax's capital at Cirta (Constantine, Algeria) and Utica. So Scipio would be able to land with his ally protecting his flank. Scipio informed his troops, not that Syphax had betrayed him, but was demanding his presence in Africa. It also meant that his enemies in the senate did not have any reason to question his suitability to command the operation.

Scipio had a large fleet of warships and transport assembled at Lilybaeum and sailed in the summer for North Africa, making land close to Cape Apollo (possibly Cap Farina) not far from the city of Utica. Near the landing site a large fort was built named after his father, the Castra Cornelius, its walls extended to cover the harbour area to protect the fleet from land attack. He then laid siege to Utica, while sending out his cavalry to drive the local population away and remove any goods of use to his army. Masinissa arrived shortly after the landing with his Numidian cavalry. Carthage reacted quickly and its scouts soon located the site of landing. Hasdrubal, who was with Syphax, was ordered to bring all available forces including Syphax's to intercept Scipio's army.

A force was dispatched from Carthage to defend the town of Salaeca 15 miles from Utica, led by a certain Hanno. Scipio sent Masinissa and his cavalry to taunt the garrison to come out and fight, while Scipio moved his cavalry up to the position as quickly as he could. The tactic worked, Hanno was lured out and charged straight into Scipio's force and was destroyed; Hanno and a number of the ruling class's sons were killed in the battle.

Days after Scipio began his siege of Utica, Hasdrubal and Syphax finally reached the area. Scipio halted the siege and moved his army back inside his fortress. Once it became obvious that Hasdrubal was unwilling to take to the field in the late autumn, Scipio returned to besieging Utica. During this time the Roman fleet resupplied his base from Sicily and Sardinia, giving him enough supplies to survive the winter in camp. Scipio now had a solid base to operate from in North Africa, but he had failed to take Utica, which would have given him a much stronger foothold. But the Carthaginians had failed to push him back into the sea. For Carthage the situation was dire, a Roman army had safely landed in North Africa, set up camp and now directly threatened the city itself.

Italy summer and autumn 204

Sempronius had also been busy and retaken the town of Clampetia, as well as the towns of Consentia and Pandosia (Tursi), which had surrendered without a fight. He had then clashed with Hannibal close to Croton; his objective was to keep Hannibal in one place while the pro-consul Licinius reached his location, so doubling the size of his army. Hannibal was sitting around waiting and forced Sempronius to retire from the field; but Hannibal stayed put and Licinius arrived. The joint army then attacked Hannibal forcing him from the field and into the city of Croton.

In Etruria, Cornelius spent the summer conducting a 'witch hunt' of any of the Etrurian nobility who were suspected of harbouring anti-Roman sentiment. Those who could, fled into exile, while those caught seemed to have been executed. Rome still feared that her 'ally' was still harbouring intent to join with Mago Barca and fight Rome.

In Rome a new temple was under construction on the Palatine to house the great Mother Goddess. The census was also announced giving Rome a male citizen population of 214,000![27]

In the winter the consul Cornelius conducted the elections for the consularship; Gnaeus Servilius Caepio and Gaius Servilius Geminus were elected, while Publius Cornelius Lentulus, Publius Quinctilius Varus, Publius Aelius Paetus and Publius Villius Tappulus were made praetors elect.

Spring 203

The 16th year of the war began for Rome with victory in sight, it would, to a large degree depend on two things. First, how Scipio conducted the campaign in Africa and secondly, how Carthage would react to the battle.

The pro-consul Cornelius took over in Cisalpine Gaul from Scribonius, Sempronius' army was handed over to Caepio and the forces of Cornelius in Etruria were handed over to Geminus. Rome was now beginning the slow campaign to regain control of Cisalpine Gaul and punish those tribes that had supported Hannibal and company, as well as rebuilding the colonies that had either been abandoned or damaged during the war.

The praetor Paetus was based in Rome and ordered to raise 2 new legions, Lentulus was sent to Sardinia, and Villius to Sicily; with orders to raise replacement troops for the men Scipio had taken to

---

[27] This shows the inherent problem of relying on data supplied by historians writing in this period. The male population has grown by at least 50% in less than 10 years.

Africa. Lucretius was sent to Genoa to guard it and begin rebuilding following its sacking by Mago Barca. Scipio's command was also renewed. The senate and consuls also decided to strength the Italian fleet and ordered new ships to be based in groups of 30-40 at ports along the coast; most likely along those that could be visited by the Carthaginians. In total the Roman war fleet numbered 160 with 20 legions in total for the year 203.

Carthage 203

Hasdrubal and Syphax remained in their camps during the winter, their purpose appears to have been not to relieve Utica, but block Scipio from advancing on Carthage. In Carthage a new fleet was equipped, with the intention of blockading Scipio at Utica with the support of Hasdrubal to destroy him there. During the early spring Syphax became an intermediary between Scipio, Hasdrubal and Carthage. Both sides appeared to have been playing for time. Scipio did not want the war to end without at least one big victory; how else was he to recover the cost of the campaign and reward his troops, Let alone treat the people of Rome to a couple of days of triumphant games. He had Hasdrubal waiting for the fleet to keep him on guard; all the time Carthage could recruit more soldiers to fight Scipio. Eventually Carthage offered Scipio (Rome) terms for ending the war; Carthage would recall the Bacrid brothers from Italy and Scipio would leave Africa.

Once Scipio had received supplies from Rome in the spring, he mounted a night attack against both Syphax and Hasdrubal's camps. The results were better than expected; as both camps were destroyed, forcing both commanders to retire inland onto the Great Plains. This worked in bringing Scipio away from Carthage and instead they based close to Obba (Ebba in Tunisia). Carthage sent them reinforcements; Syphax also received more Numidian recruits. Scipio brought his forces to Obba and both forces clashed. Scipio used the normal Roman formation; the infantry in the centre, with Masinissa and his cavalry on the left and on the right allied cavalry under Scipio. Scipio's cavalry, along with Masinissa, dispersed the Carthaginians and Syphax's cavalry. Scipio and his troops were able to move in behind the Carthaginian infantry and the Romans chewed up what was left of both sides. Syphax fled with his surviving troops back to his capital of Cirta, pursued by Masinissa and Laelius with allied cavalry and Velites. Hasdrubal, with his survivors reached Carthage.

Scipio, after collecting the spoils, retired back to Utica to continue with the siege, then, with enough troops left in place to continue the siege, he advanced on Carthage and took Tunis. Carthage dispatched ships to Italy with orders to bring Hannibal and his brother Mago home to defend Carthage.

Masinissa and Laelius caught up with Syphax close to Cirta and defeated him as well as his remaining forces; capturing Syphax alive. Masinissa, with Syphax in tow, headed into Cirta which surrendered to him and he proclaimed himself king in place of Syphax. He proceeded to take Syphax's wife Sophonisba into his custody. Livy (1965) now had Sophonisba, the daughter of Hasdrubal, play the eastern temptress; using her sexual wiles she made Masinissa break faith with Scipio by marrying her, instead of handing her and Syphax over to Scipio as Roman prisoners. Secondly Livy shows how easily non-Romans, especially Numidians, were lured away from duty by lust etc... overall how they were very 'un-Roman'. Masinissa also promised Sophonisba that he would never allow her to become a prisoner and get taken to Rome in chains. Here, Livy is casting Sophonisba as a Carthaginian Cleopatra; using her sexual wiles to beguile the once loyal allies of Rome. He sent Syphax back to Scipio.

In the meantime Carthage launched its counter attack against Scipio without the land forces to support the navy. The Carthaginian fleet managed to break up the Roman transports being used to besiege Utica and managed to drag away a number of them as trophies for Carthage. But they failed to break the siege and Utica was left surrounded by Scipio's forces.

Syphax, with his ex-wife Sophonisba, Masinissa and Laelius reached Scipio's camp. Livy (1965) then had Scipio interview his once faithful ally Syphax in an effort to understand why he betrayed him and Rome. Livy[28] again uses recent Roman history as a way to explain what had happened, but also as a tool to remind his readers of the recent triumph of Augustus against his once noble ally Mark Anthony. Syphax relates how it was all the fault of the eastern beauty Sophonisba, she had used her charms to draw him away from Scipio and Rome and form an alliance with their mortal enemy Carthage. Again, Livy has Sophonisba play Cleopatra and Syphax the role of Mark Antony, while Scipio is Augustus; the calm and reserved Roman who never betrays his duty to his natural urges etc... to end the story Masinissa sent poison to his new wife so she could escape the fate of a prisoner dragged to Rome. She, like Cleopatra, happily took the poison and so escaped the fate of a captive; it worked so that Masinissa could also keep his word to her. With the matter over, Scipio again trusted Masinissa as his ally. Laelius, with Syphax and loot in tow, was then sent back to Rome to announce the conquest of this Numidian kingdom.

Scipio returned to Tunis and set up camp. The senate of Carthage decided that the war was over and sent envoys to Scipio to request an armistice, as well as to discuss peace terms. Scipio, acting on behalf of Rome, agreed to the armistice probably around late summer, so the rest offered by the armistice could be put to use resupplying his army etc... Scipio informed the envoys that his terms for peace were the payment of the costs of the invasion of North Africa, the return of all Roman and allied prisoners and deserters, that Hannibal and Mago were to leave Europe and that Carthage would be allowed to keep 20 warships, but the rest were to be handed over to Rome. The envoys agreed and Scipio sent them to Rome for the senate and the people to agree to the terms.

For Carthage the war appeared to be over and Scipio also assumed the same.

Liguria 203

Mago Barca was heavily defeated by Cornelius and Varus and was also wounded in the battle. He retired back to the coast close to Genoa, and what remained of his forces were picked up by the ships sent from Carthage. However, on the return journey they were intercepted by one of the Roman fleets; Mago Barca was killed and the fleet destroyed. Rome had now defeated the threat from the north; it is probable that neither Mago nor the Roman fleet were aware of the armistice in North Africa, as the envoys did not seem to have reached Rome until after the event. The consul Servilius also managed to rescue his father and Gaius Catullus from the Boii who had held them since 218 BC. Because of this the senate had to pass a special dispensation bill for Servilius; as he had broken Roman custom and law in becoming a magistrate without his father's permission (even though it was assumed at the time that his father was dead) and that was that.

---

[28] Livy wasn't alone in portraying Augustus as a historical Roman figure; Virgil also portrays Augustus as Aeneas. Both owed their rise to Augustus in the period, as he was the great patron of the era

Bruttium summer 203

Geminus did his duty and kept Hannibal inside Croton until the Carthaginian fleet arrived and removed Hannibal and part of his army. The remaining troops were left to guard what was left of Hannibal's conquests in Bruttium. Geminus was then actually criticised for not fulfilling his duty and keeping Hannibal in Croton, thereby allowing him to leave.

The news reached Rome of the death of Mago and Hannibal's retreat from Croton at about the same time that Laelius arrived with news from Scipio. The senate, overjoyed, proclaimed 5 days of celebration for the city of Rome; offerings were made to all the gods, stewing couches placed in the temples and animals sacrificed. In the autumn the peace envoys from Carthage reached Rome and the senate conducted a hearing; they seemed to have accepted the terms Scipio had already agreed. So the war seemed to be over at last.

Autumn Carthage 203

One of the fleets bringing supplies to Scipio was caught in a storm and part of the fleet made land close to Carthage. The Carthaginians believed that it was a Roman invasion fleet and that Rome had broken the armistice; so they sailed out and captured the ships thus breaking the peace. Scipio demanded the ships returned or the truce was formally broken and Carthage refused; probably about the same time as news reached the city that Hannibal and his troops had reached Leptis. The peace envoys arrived back to find themselves back in the war.

Scipio and his forces wintered at Tunis and outside Utica.

Winter 203

News reached Rome that Philip V had broken the treaty with them; sending reinforcements and money to Carthage, as well as raiding some of Rome's Greek allies. A deputation was prepared to sail as soon as weather permitted them to leave; to visit Greece, confront Philip V and the allies to determine the truth of the accusations.

The elections were held, with Tiberius Claudius Nero and Marcus Servilius elected consuls, Sabinus, Flaccus, Gaius Salinatus and Gaius Aurelius Cotta as Praetors elect.

Quintus Fabius died and was given the title Maximus 'the great', the Roman poet Ennius wrote a short verse of poetry in which it states "one man by his delaying tactics saved the state", so Fabius collected the title the 'delayer' *Cunctator*.

Spring 202

With the departure of Hannibal and Mago, the senate and the consuls were now able to reduce the number of legions to 16. Scipio's command was renewed, although Livy (1965) hints that the consul, T Claudius Nero, attempted to gain joint command so that he could share in the glory of victory; whilst his colleague Servilius was dispatched to Etruria to continue with the campaign of reconquering Cisalpine Gaul. G. Servilius had his command extended along with Sextus, who moved to support the consul in Cisalpine Gaul; taking two legions from Varus. Livius took command of the army of Sempronius in Bruttium and the praetors were now assigned to Sicily, Sardinia, northern Italy and the city praetorship. Pomponius was ordered back to Rome with 20 ships.

Gradually the Roman war machine was winding down and it was also slowly removing those senior magistrates from positions of command. But an unfortunate precedence had been set; the old method of containing the power of the consul to one year had proved to be inefficient in the war with Hannibal, and so had been extended over a period of years. That of the praetorship had also undergone this change. The elite of Rome had consolidated their control on the city and the people; led by the tribunes of the plebs, would find their role harder to act independently of the will of senate.

Carthage 202

Hannibal had wintered in Hadrumetum (Sousse) and in the spring had actively recruited more forces from Libya and the hinterland of North Africa. In the summer he went on the offensive, taking the inland shorter route (rather than the longer coastal) to Scipio; so that he would appear from the south and strike Scipio in the rear at Utica or Tunis. Scipio learned of his movements and moved most of his army to intercept him, both armies met at Zama, or close to the city of Naraggara. Livy (1965) has Hannibal demand a meeting with Scipio the day before the battle. Livy uses the 'meeting' as a chance to compare the two greatest commanders of the period; Hannibal is described as essentially a broken man who would rather sue for a just peace than fight, while Scipio is the youthful, just, proud Roman soldier whose duty is to destroy the threat of Hannibal permanently and so refuses peace and opts for war.

Scipio changed the normal formation of the Roman infantry in the centre; by breaking up the three divisions into their separate maniples, leaving gaps on either side of each maniple. This allowed each maniple a greater flexibility in reacting to threats and also stopped the whole formation from being bunched up, as had happened at Cannae. Scipio was not going to allow Hannibal any chance of compacting the Roman infantry. In gaps in the front line, he placed his Velites, who could move in and out of the gaps as required. On the right wing he placed Masinissa and his Numidians and, on his left, he placed the allied cavalry under Laelius.

Hannibal again adopted Roman tactics and laid out his infantry into three ranks. In the front he placed his Ligurian, Gallic, Mauritanian and Balearics troops; in the second rank his Carthaginian, Libyan and the Macedonian troops from Philip, in the last his southern Italian troops who had crossed with him. Hannibal's main advantage was that most of his army had nowhere to go if they lost the battle; the Italians for one knew that Scipio would show no mercy to them if they were captured, so he expected that most of his army would fight to the death. On his right wing he placed his Carthaginian cavalry and on his left Numidian cavalry still loyal to Syphax. Lastly, in front of his army he placed his elephants whose task was to break up the Roman infantry formations.

Scipio attacked first; sending his cavalry to contain Hannibal's; in this they were singularly very successful. Hannibal struck back by sending forth the elephants while his army advanced. Scipio's open formation defeated the purpose of the elephants, which were then driven back into Hannibal's front line. Both armies clashed, the Roman infantry once again proved how effective they were and combined with Masinissa and Laelius' cavalry; striking from the rear gave Hannibal the experience of the type of defeat he had inflicted on Rome at Cannae. So Scipio had performed a reverse Cannae and for the first time a Roman general had not only totally defeated Hannibal, but had done it on Hannibal's home ground. Hannibal fled back to Hadrumetum; he could not reach Carthage by land as Scipio was holding the landward end of the peninsula Carthage lay on. He eventually reached the city by ship.

Scipio remained on the battlefield while his army looted the dead and Hannibal's camp, before moving back to Tunis to prepare for the assault on the city of Carthage. Laelius was dispatched back to Rome to inform the senate of the victory and likely fall of Carthage.

Scipio began operations to attack Carthage in the late autumn, as Livy (1965) states that Syphax's son Vermina attempted to stop Scipio by attacking him outside Tunis, but was repulsed and defeated on the first of the Saturnalia (17th December 202). Shortly after this a senior delegation approached Scipio and asked for an armistice so they could hold peace talks.

Scipio set out his terms for peace with Rome:

1. Carthage would only be allowed to have a fleet of ten warships, the remainder were to be handed over to Rome
2. They were no longer to use war elephants; all were to be given to Rome
3. All prisoners were to be returned, runaway slaves and, most importantly, all Roman and allied deserters were to be handed over
4. Carthage would be allowed to retain its North African processions
5. Carthage would become an ally of Rome and only be allowed to wage war with the express permission of the senate of Rome
6. They would have to pay, over a 50-year period, 10,000 talents of silver as compensation for waging war against Rome
7. Hostages chosen from the elite of Carthage were to be sent to Rome
8. All Roman war materials captured (ships etc...) were to be returned
9. And the costs of the Roman expeditionary force to be paid straight away in sliver.

Carthage accepted these terms and the delegation was then sent on to Rome for the senate and the people to agree to the terms Scipio had set out.

Italy autumn 202

The consul Claudius attempted to reach Scipio, but his fleet was caught in a storm and he was stranded, the consul Servilius was also unable to reach Rome in time for the elections, so nominated G. Servilius Geminus to act as dictator and hold the elections; but he was unable to reach Rome before after the ides of March in 201. So for the first time Rome was unable to elect its consuls or praetors for the following year.

Spring 201

On the 14th March, the consuls, praetors and fellow magistrates resigned as normal, leaving the city without any magistrates. The envoys from Carthage reached Rome and were seen by the senate, envoys from Philip V also arrived; but no talks could occur until the election had taken place. Lucius Philo gave a report to the senate first and then to the people in the forum, of the victory of Scipio against Hannibal and the subsequent ending of the war. Three days of public thanks to the gods followed, using 'stewing couches' and sacrifices.

The elections were finally held; Gnaeus Cornelius Lentulus and Publius Aelius Paetus were made consuls. With new praetors including Marcus Pennus as city praetor, Marcus Falto sent to Bruttium, Marcus Buteo to Sardinia and Publius Tubero to Sicily. Lentulus was assigned to Africa to command the fleet and Paetus had the whole of Italy. Scipio was left in command of the army outside Carthage. In Spain the army was disbanded and its commanders Lentulus and Acidinus brought home with the demobbed troops. New commanders were appointed for Spain with orders to raise a new army. Rome now reduced its army to 14 legions and a fleet of 100 ships.

The envoys of Philip V were interviewed in the presence of the senators who had been to Greece to investigate Philip's conduct. The senate found Philip guilty of breaking the treaty with them and sent a warning that his conduct would most likely lead to war with Rome.

Finally the envoys from Carthage were seen and the senate voted to accept the terms given by Scipio; at which point the consul Lentulus vetoed it. The only reason for this could be that he would be unable to jointly celebrate the victory with Scipio, as the peace was agreed before he could take up his command in Africa. So the tribunes of plebs took the matter to the people, who no doubt were sick of the war; as they were the ones whose sons, fathers and brothers had been away doing the fighting, so cancelling the consul's veto. Rome was officially at peace again with Carthage after 17 years of war.

Once the envoys returned to Carthage, the city quickly abided by the terms and handed over all its prisoners to Scipio; who sent them back to Rome. The allied deserters were beheaded and all Roman deserters were crucified outside Carthage. The slaves were sent back either to their masters or sold off for profit by Scipio. He then destroyed the Carthaginian fleet, as Rome had no need of it. Masinissa was now officially given Syphax's kingdom as an ally of Rome, which meant that Rome leased him the kingdom in exchange for his continued support; he was now an allied subject or client king of the developing Roman Empire.

Scipio returned to Rome with the loot and was given a triumph; he paid for the celebration games that followed, he also paid each of his soldiers a bonus and deposited a very large sum in the treasury as gift to the gods.

The Second Punic War was over.

Epilogue

Scipio remained in public office till 184, when he was forced to quit; after continuous attacks concerning his supposed rejection of traditional Roman values and adoption of Hellenic dress, attitudes and lifestyle by Cato the Censor. Rome, following its intervention in Greece, developed a real taste for all things Hellenic[29], while Cato the Censor became the voice of those who believed that what had made, and would make, Rome great were the traditional Roman values of moderation in lifestyle. So in this period Latin, as opposed to Greek, was favoured in writing and poetry thereby developing a Roman heritage, as opposed to a perceived foreign Hellenic one.

In 200 BC Rome went to war with Philip V and he was finally defeated by the consul T Quinctius Flaminius at Cynoscephalae in 197 BC, and then became an active ally of Rome in the region.

Hannibal remained in Carthage until he fled in 195 BC to the Hellenic court of Antiochus III (the great) Seleucid ruler of Syria, who was at the time planning to go to war with Rome in Greece. He was heavily defeated at the battle of Magnesia (Manisa, Turkey) by the brothers Scipio and Attalus' son Eumenes II in 190; forcing Hannibal to flee to Bithynia, where he eventually committed suicide, rather than fall into the hands of Rome in either 182/1 BC.

In 150 BC the Third and final Punic War broke out, caused by Carthage intervening in Masinissa's affairs in Numidia, so breaking the terms of the treaty according to the likes of Cato the Censor (who had been demanding war with Carthage for years)

In 146 BC the Roman army stormed into the city under the command of Scipio Aemilianus (adopted grandson of Scipio) and destroyed the city of Carthage for good.

---

[29] Rome had always been deeply influenced by the Greeks, from use of the phalanx to the adoption of the Greek gods.

Appendix One

Plutarch on Fabius:

Plutarch's (2001) aim in writing his 'Lives' was to compare, in most cases, a Roman historical figure with a comparable Greek figure. It was not meant to be a historical account of their lives, but more a judgement by Plutarch on how they lived their lives and what made them great or bad. So, it is full of anecdotes or short stories that are meant to enliven the account and give access to the inner workings of the person in question.

In the case of Fabius, Plutarch compared him with the great Athenian Pericles. Most of Plutarch's material is drawn from Livy and Polybius' accounts, which he then edits to bring out, as he sees it, the aspects of Fabius' actions that so impress him. Therefore the Second Punic War is just a backdrop in which Fabius appears. For example, the battle of Cannae is only mentioned briefly, chiefly because Paulus was a friend of Fabius and died in that battle. He then, after praising him, condemns him for attempting to stop Scipio from invading North Africa. Plutarch attempts to present, as he would have seen it, a balanced account of Fabius' life; good and bad.

It is in the direct comparison between Fabius and Pericles that Plutarch is at his finest and asks a question which is still relevant.

Is a leader who is called to save his country (Fabius in this case), the better man for the role of leader, or is the man who strives for and obtains the role (Pericles) the better suited for the role?

He leaves the reader to judge who is the better leader.

Bibliography

Bagnall, N., 2002. *The Punic wars 264-146 BC - Essential Histories 16.* 2009 ed. Oxford: Osprey Publishing Ltd.

Chowaniec, d. R., 2012. *Akrai Archaeological Mission.* [Online]
Available at: http://www.akrai.uw.edu.pl/index.php
[Accessed August 2012].

Duncan B Campbell, I. A. H., 2005. *Siege Warfare in the Roman World 146 BC - AD 378.* 2008 ed. Oxford: Osprey Publishing Ltd.

Hook, D. B. C. -. I. b. A., 2005. *Ancient Siege Warfare Persians, Greeks, Carthaginians and Romans 546-146 BC - Elite 121.* 2008 ed. Oxford: Osprey Publishing Ltd.

Keppie, L., 1998. *The Making of the Roman Army.* 2003 ed. London: Routledge.

Livy, 1965. *The War with Hannibal - Books XXI-XXX of The History of Rome from its Foundation Translated by Aubrey de Selincourt.* 1972 ed. London: Penguin Books.

Miles, R., 2011. *CARTHAGE MUST BE DESTROYED The Rise And Fall of an Ancient Civilization.* 2011 ed. London: Penguin Books.

Morstein-Marx, E. b. N. R. a. R., 2010. *A Companion To The Roman Republic.* 1st ed. Chichester: Blackwell Publishing Ltd.

Moscati, S., 1968. *The World of the Phoenicians.* Cardinal, 1973 ed. London: Sphere Books Ltd.

Multo, 2012. *Wikipedia l'enciclopedia libera.* [Online]
Available at: http://it.wikipedia.org/wiki/Pagina_principale
[Accessed August 2012].

Plutarch, 2001. *Plutarch's Lives Volume 1, The Dryden Translation, edited with notes and preface by Arthur Hugh Clough.* 1st ed. New York: Modern Library Paperback Edition, Random House Inc.

Polybius, 2010. *The Histories - A new translation by Robin Waterfield.* Oxford World's Classics 1st edition ed. Oxford: Oxford University Press.

Sciarretta, A., 2002. *Antonio Sciarretta's Toponymy.* [Online]
Available at: http://asciatopo.xoom.it/index.html
[Accessed August 2012].

Printed in Great Britain
by Amazon.co.uk, Ltd.,
Marston Gate.